Storytime Origami

John Montroll

Dover Publications, Inc.
New York

To Brian, Erica, Kira, Selena, and Jana

Bibliographical Note

This work is first published in 2009 in separate editions by Antroll Publishing Company, Maryland, and Dover Publications, Inc., Mineola, New York.

Library of Congress Cataloging-in-Publication Data

Montroll, John.
   Storytime origami / John Montroll.
      p. cm.
   ISBN 978-0-486-46786-3
   1. Origami. I. Title.
TT870.M5738 2009
736'.982—dc22

                                                        2009004140

      Manufactured in the United States of America
Dover Publications, Inc., 31 East 2nd Street, Mineola, N.Y. 11501

Storytime Origami

Other books by John Montroll:

Origami Sculptures

Origami Sea Life by John Montroll and Robert J. Lang

North American Animals in Origami

Teach Yourself Origami

Bringing Origami to Life

Dollar Bill Animals in Origami

Bugs and Birds in Origami

Dollar Bill Origami

A Constellation of Origami Polyhedra

Christmas Origami

Animal Origami for the Enthusiast

Origami for the Enthusiast

Easy Origami

Birds in Origami

Favorite Animals in Origami

Easy Christmas Origami

Introduction

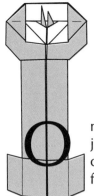

Once upon a time, a pumpkin turned into a carriage and the bowl of porridge was just right. Throughout the years, generations have enjoyed retelling the classic childrens' stories like Cinderella and The Three Bears, stories that take us to faraway lands.

Now you can fold scenes for The Ugly Duckling, The Three Bears, The Three Little Pigs, Humpty Dumpty, and Cinderella in this collection of 42 original origami models. The stories themselves are also included. From the wicked stepmother to Cinderella, bowls of porridge, tables, chairs, and beds for the Three Bears, straw house and wolf, these origami projects will provide hours of enjoyment.

Most of the models are of intermediate level with a few simple and low complex ones. The difficulty level is shown in the contents. Folders of all abilities will enjoy the variety of animals, humans, plants, and objects in this collection.

Each model is folded from a single sheet of uncut paper. The illustrations conform to the internationally accepted Randlett-Yoshizawa conventions. The colored side of origami paper is represented by the shadings in the diagrams. Origami paper can be found in many hobby shops or purchased by mail from OrigamiUSA, 15 West 77th Street, New York, NY 10024-5192 or from Dover Publications, Inc., 31 East 2nd Street, Mineola, NY 11501. Large sheets are easier to use than small ones.

Many people helped with this project. I thank my editors, Jan Polish and Charley Montroll. I also thank Charley Montroll for writing the stories. I give thanks to Brian Webb for his support throughout this project. And I thank the many folders who proofread the diagrams.

John Montroll

www.johnmontroll.com

Contents

★ Simple
★★ Intermediate
★★★ Complex

The Ugly Duckling   *page 12*

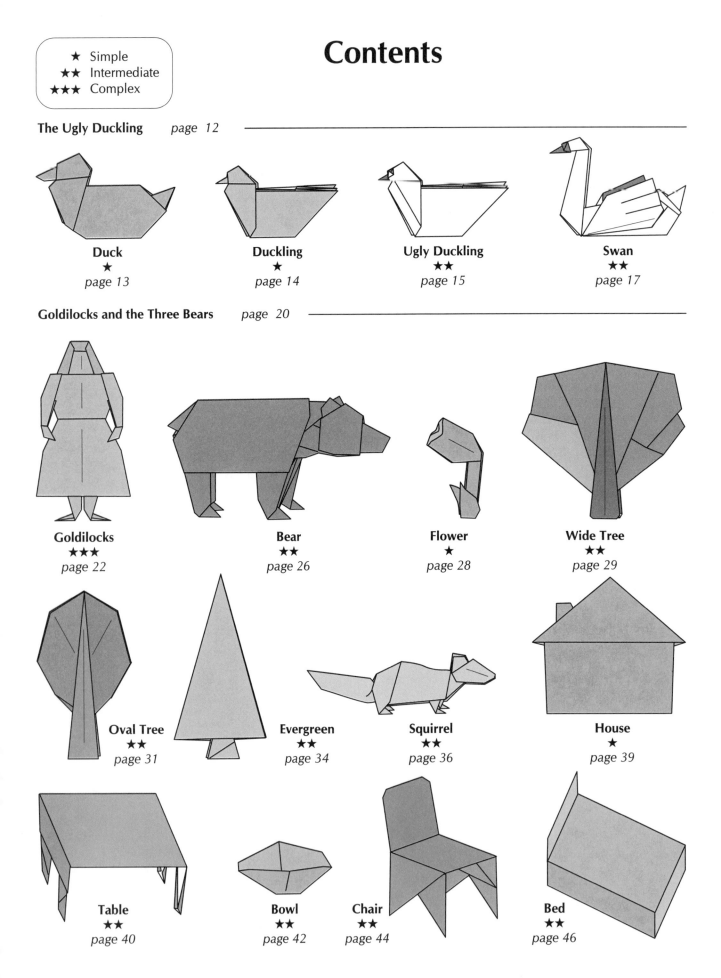

Duck
★
page 13

Duckling
★
page 14

Ugly Duckling
★★
page 15

Swan
★★
page 17

Goldilocks and the Three Bears   *page 20*

Goldilocks
★★★
page 22

Bear
★★
page 26

Flower
★
page 28

Wide Tree
★★
page 29

Oval Tree
★★
page 31

Evergreen
★★
page 34

Squirrel
★★
page 36

House
★
page 39

Table
★★
page 40

Bowl
★★
page 42

Chair
★★
page 44

Bed
★★
page 46

The Three Little Pigs   *page 51*

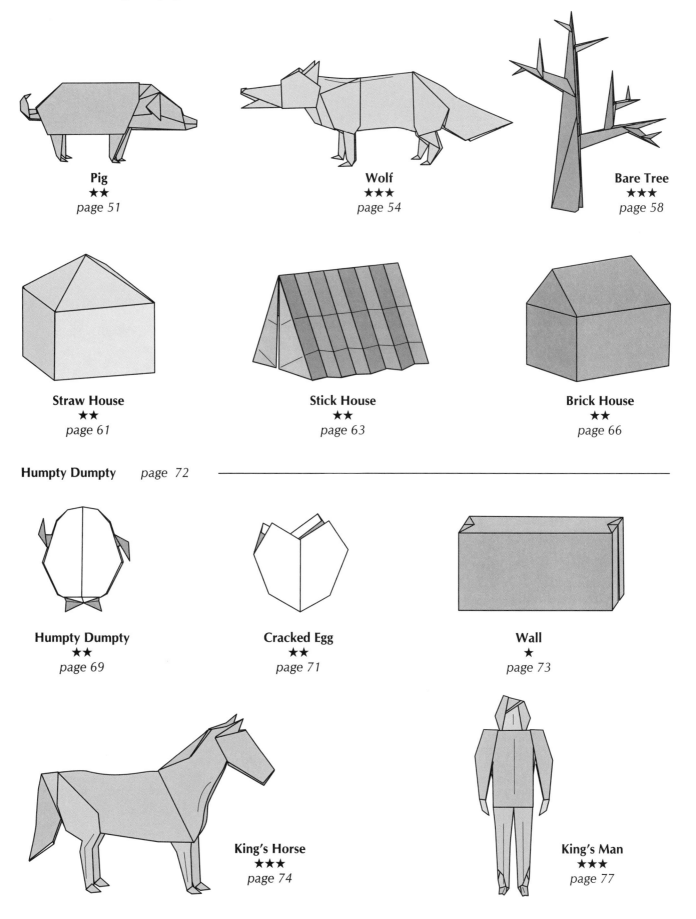

Pig
★★
page 51

Wolf
★★★
page 54

Bare Tree
★★★
page 58

Straw House
★★
page 61

Stick House
★★
page 63

Brick House
★★
page 66

Humpty Dumpty   *page 72*

Humpty Dumpty
★★
page 69

Cracked Egg
★★
page 71

Wall
★
page 73

King's Horse
★★★
page 74

King's Man
★★★
page 77

Contents 7

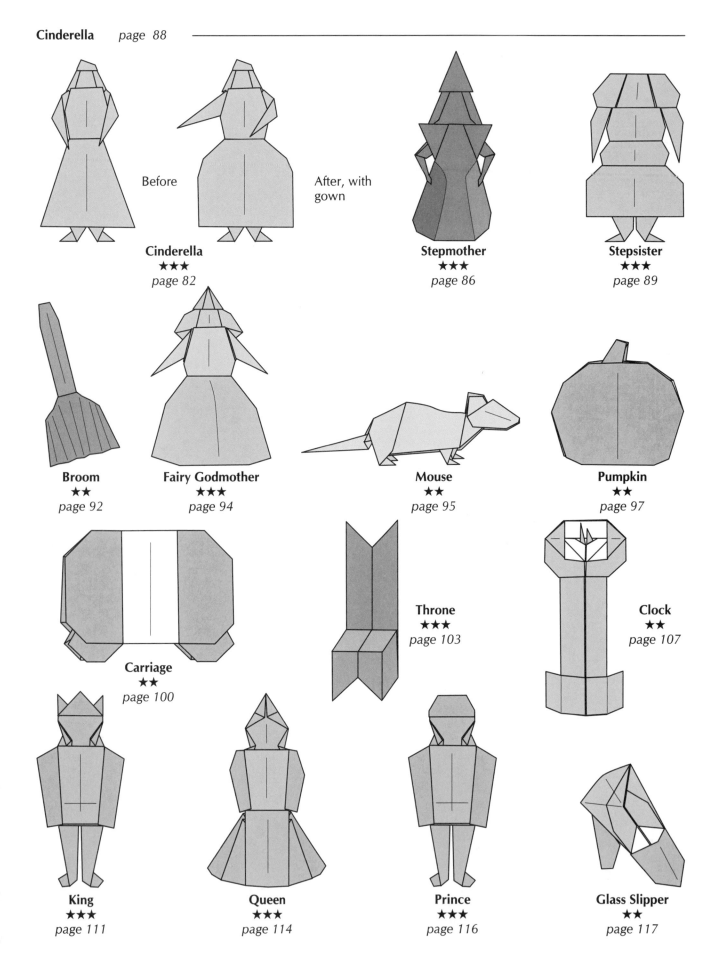

Before

After, with gown

Cinderella
★★★
page 82

Stepmother
★★★
page 86

Stepsister
★★★
page 89

Broom
★★
page 92

Fairy Godmother
★★★
page 94

Mouse
★★
page 95

Pumpkin
★★
page 97

Carriage
★★
page 100

Throne
★★★
page 103

Clock
★★
page 107

King
★★★
page 111

Queen
★★★
page 114

Prince
★★★
page 116

Glass Slipper
★★
page 117

Symbols

Lines

– – – – – – – – –   Valley fold, fold in front.

–·–·–·–·–·–   Mountain fold, fold behind.

———————   Crease line.

····························   X-ray or guide line.

Arrows

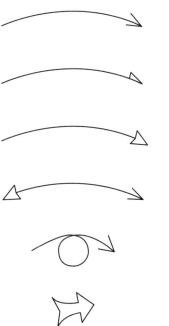 Fold in this direction.

Fold behind.

Unfold.

Fold and unfold.

Turn over.

Sink or three dimensional folding.

 Place your finger between these layers.

Basic Folds

Rabbit Ear.

To fold a rabbit ear, one corner is
folded in half and laid down to a side.

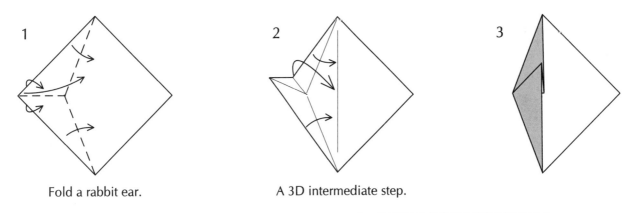

1

2

3

Fold a rabbit ear.

A 3D intermediate step.

Squash Fold.

In a squash fold, some paper is opened
and then made flat. The shaded arrow
shows where to place your finger.

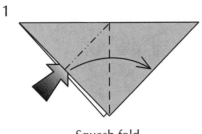
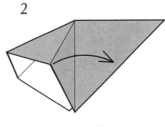
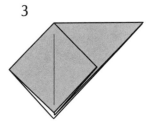

1

2

3

Squash-fold.

A 3D intermediate step.

Petal Fold.

In a petal fold, one point is folded up while
two opposite sides meet each other.

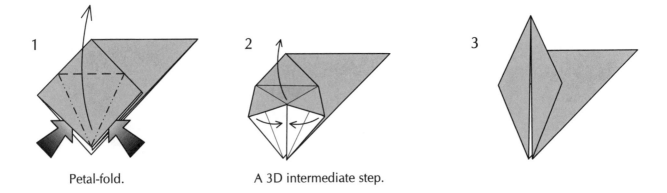

1

2

3

Petal-fold.

A 3D intermediate step.

Inside Reverse Fold.

In an inside reverse fold, some paper is folded between layers. Here are two examples.

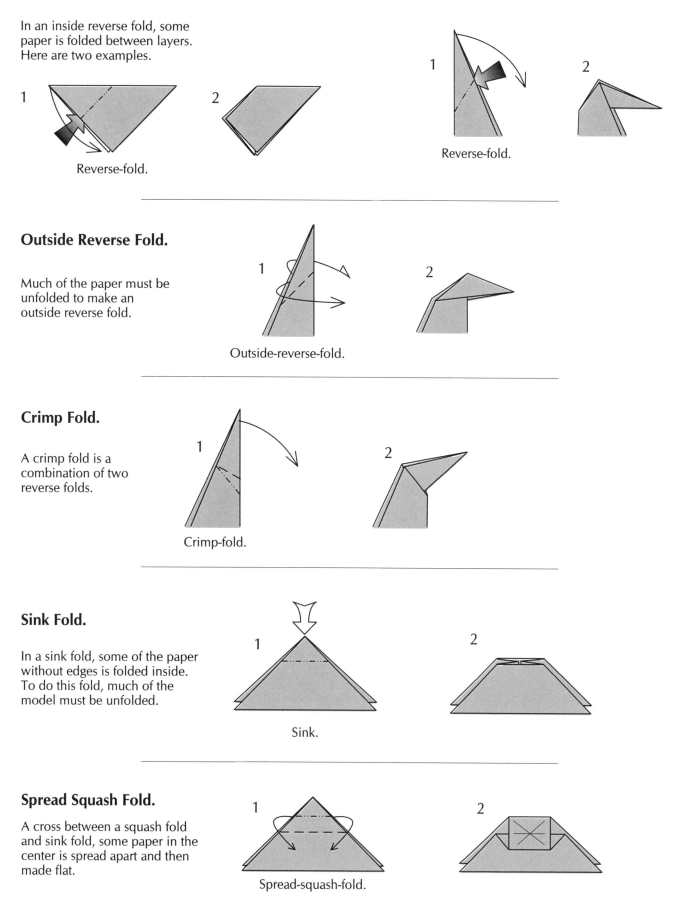

Reverse-fold.

Reverse-fold.

Outside Reverse Fold.

Much of the paper must be unfolded to make an outside reverse fold.

Outside-reverse-fold.

Crimp Fold.

A crimp fold is a combination of two reverse folds.

Crimp-fold.

Sink Fold.

In a sink fold, some of the paper without edges is folded inside. To do this fold, much of the model must be unfolded.

Sink.

Spread Squash Fold.

A cross between a squash fold and sink fold, some paper in the center is spread apart and then made flat.

Spread-squash-fold.

The Ugly Duckling

Once upon a time there was a nest by the river. In the nest were five eggs, and on the nest sat Mother Duck. The first egg hatched, and out waddled a tiny yellow duckling. The second egg hatched, and out waddled a tiny yellow duckling. Then the third egg hatched, and out waddled a tiny yellow duckling. Then the fourth egg hatched, and out waddled a tiny yellow duckling. But the last egg did not hatch, and Mother Duck sat patiently on it. Finally, the last egg hatched. To Mother Duck's surprise, out waddled, not a tiny yellow duckling, but a gray bird, much larger than the others.

Duck

Mother Duck was surprised and wondered how that happened.

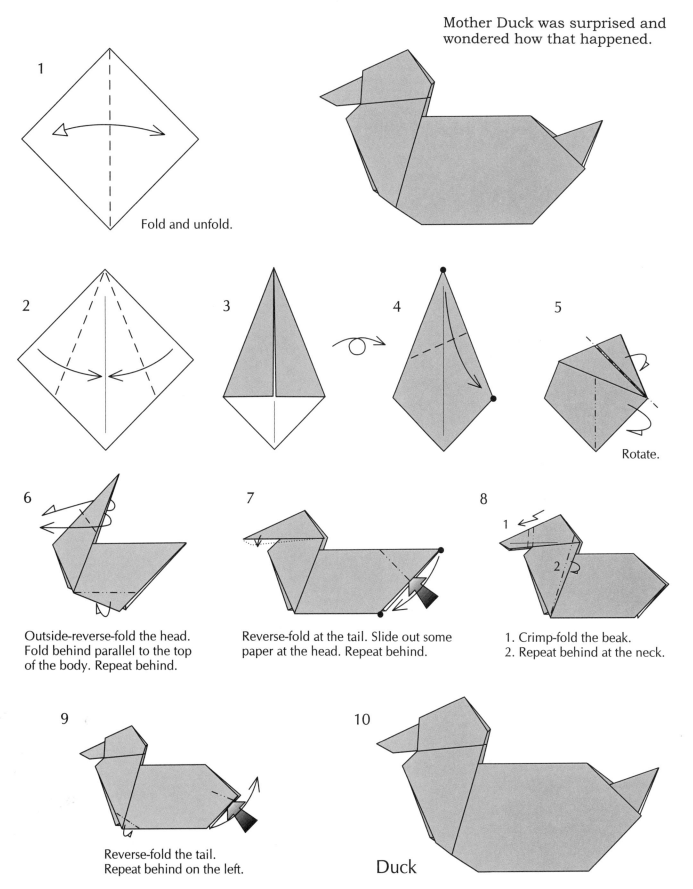

1

Fold and unfold.

2

3

4

5

Rotate.

6

Outside-reverse-fold the head.
Fold behind parallel to the top
of the body. Repeat behind.

7

Reverse-fold at the tail. Slide out some
paper at the head. Repeat behind.

8

1. Crimp-fold the beak.
2. Repeat behind at the neck.

9

Reverse-fold the tail.
Repeat behind on the left.

10

Duck

Duckling

As the ducklings grew older, they noticed that the youngest was very different from them. They were golden, but he was gray. They were beautiful and graceful, but he was ugly and gawky. The older ducklings teased him. One day a duck nearby saw this odd bird and said loudly, "What an ugly duckling!" The name stuck, and soon everyone called the gray bird "Ugly Duckling."

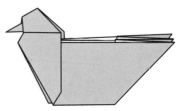

1

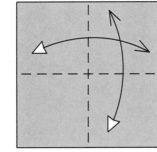

Fold and unfold.

2

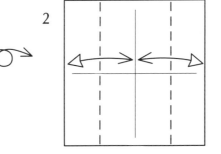

Fold and unfold.

3

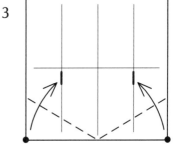

4

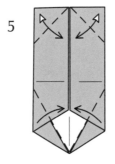

5

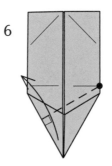

Fold and unfold on the top.

6

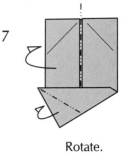

Note the right angle.

7

Rotate.

8

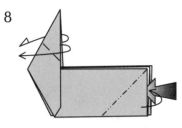

Outside-reverse-fold the head. Reverse-fold the tail and repeat behind.

9

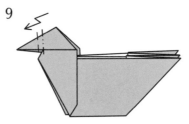

Crimp-fold the beak.

10

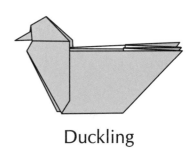

Duckling

Ugly Duckling

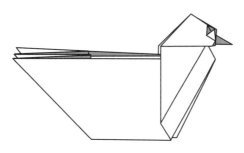

The Ugly Duckling would often wander off by himself and sigh, "I don't want to be an Ugly Duckling." But he would go back to his family, where the older ducklings would tease him again.

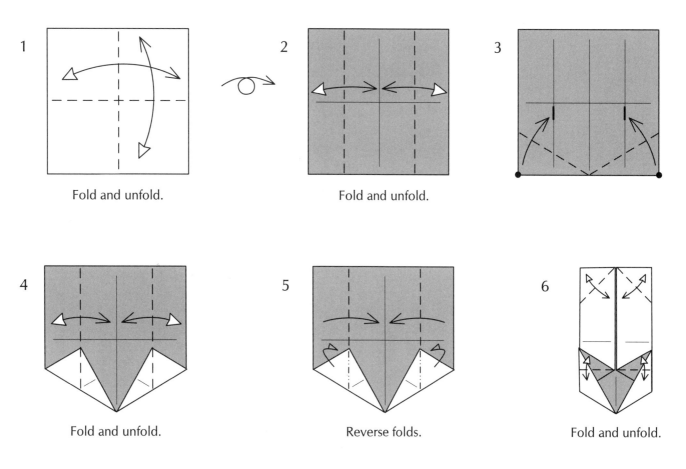

1 Fold and unfold.

2 Fold and unfold.

3

4 Fold and unfold.

5 Reverse folds.

6 Fold and unfold.

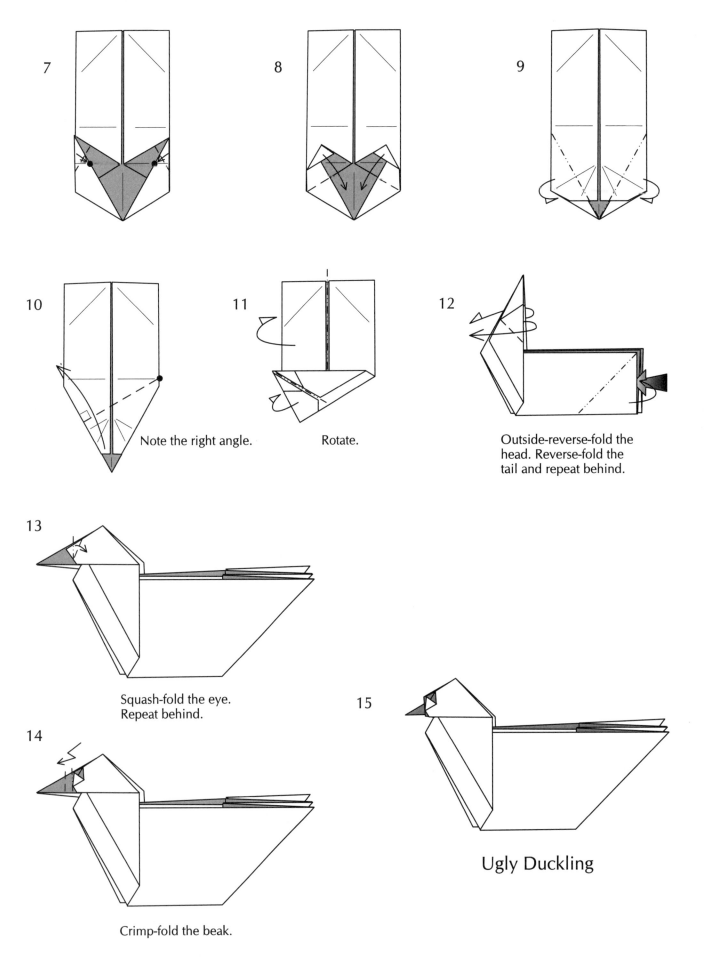

7

8

9

10

Note the right angle.

11

Rotate.

12

Outside-reverse-fold the head. Reverse-fold the tail and repeat behind.

13

Squash-fold the eye. Repeat behind.

14

Crimp-fold the beak.

15

Ugly Duckling

Swan

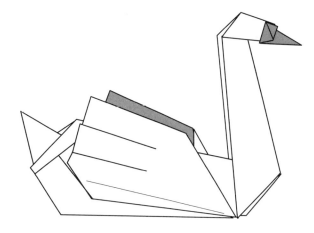

One day, the Ugly Duckling heard a glorious sound, like trumpets in the distance. Paddling their way across the pond, in a stately line, was a family of elegant long-necked white birds. The Ugly Duckling truly admired these big and graceful birds.

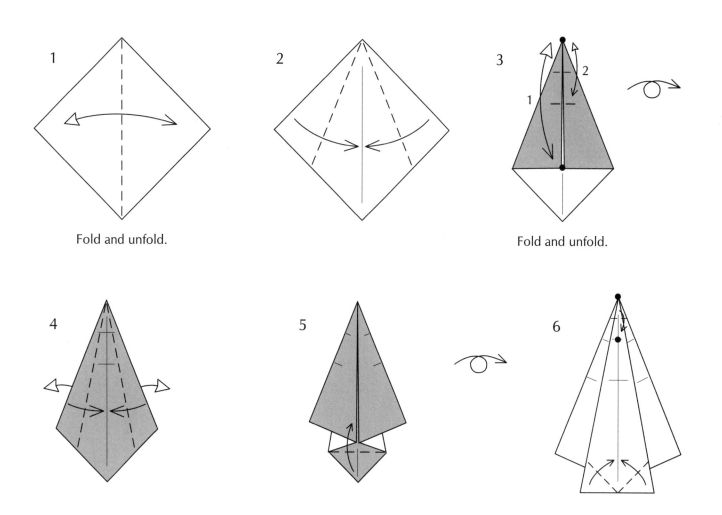

1

Fold and unfold.

2

3

Fold and unfold.

4

5

6

7

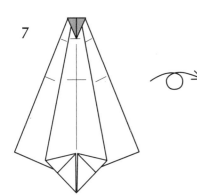

8

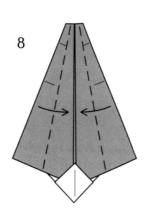

9

10

Fold and unfold.

11

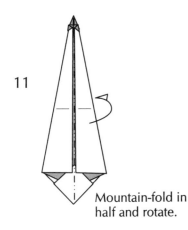

Mountain-fold in half and rotate.

12

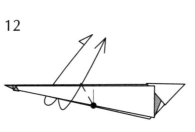

Outside-reverse-fold.

13

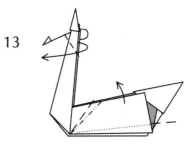

Outside-reverse-fold the head.
Fold the wing. Repeat behind.

14

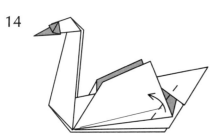

Repeat behind.

15

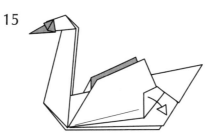

Unfold and repeat behind.

16

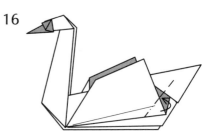

Reverse-fold and repeat behind.

17

Crimp-fold the tail. Pleat the
wing and repeat behind.

18

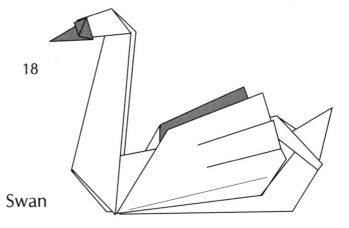

Swan

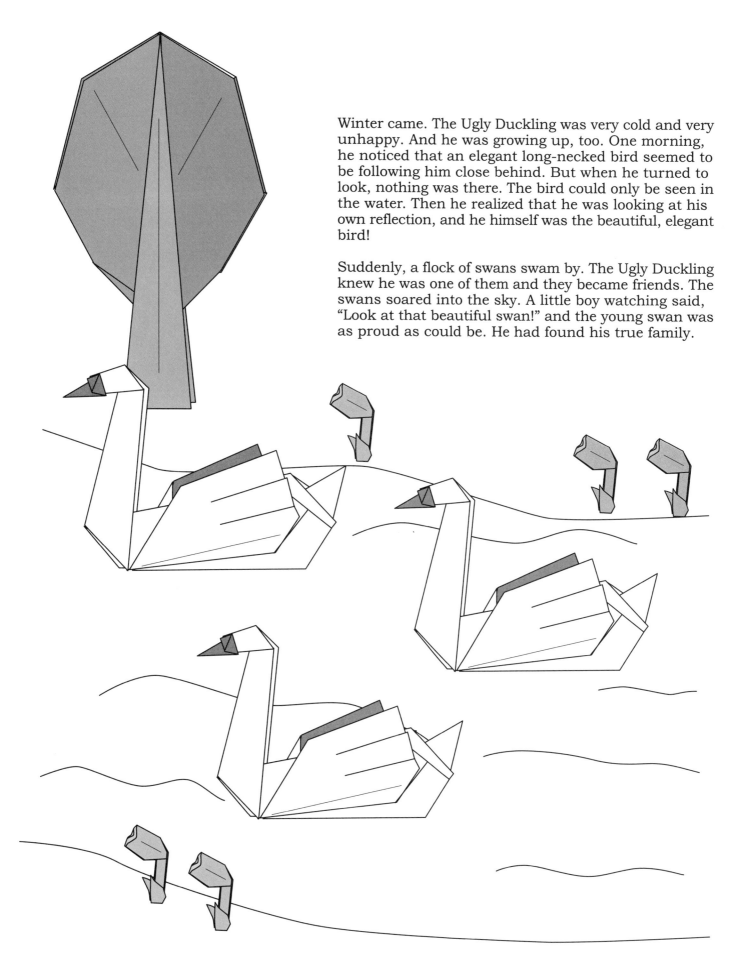

Winter came. The Ugly Duckling was very cold and very unhappy. And he was growing up, too. One morning, he noticed that an elegant long-necked bird seemed to be following him close behind. But when he turned to look, nothing was there. The bird could only be seen in the water. Then he realized that he was looking at his own reflection, and he himself was the beautiful, elegant bird!

Suddenly, a flock of swans swam by. The Ugly Duckling knew he was one of them and they became friends. The swans soared into the sky. A little boy watching said, "Look at that beautiful swan!" and the young swan was as proud as could be. He had found his true family.

Goldilocks
and the Three Bears

Once upon a time there were three bears, the Mama Bear, the Papa Bear, and the Baby Bear. At breakfast, they all sat down for their bowls of porridge. Papa Bear said "My porridge is too hot." Mama Bear said "My porridge is too hot." And Baby Bear said "My porridge is too hot." So they went out for a walk in the forest, while their porridge cooled.

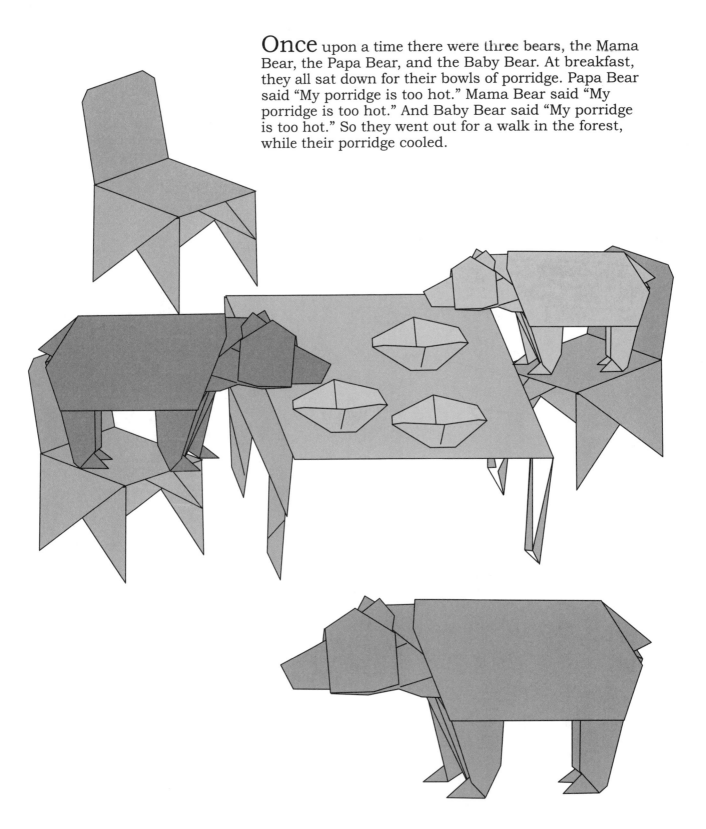

A little girl named Goldilocks was walking in the forest. Soon she came to a clearing, and in the middle of the clearing was a tiny house. She knocked on the door but there was no answer. She knocked and knocked again. Still no answer, so she went in.

Goldilocks

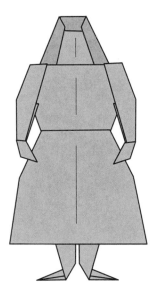

Goldilocks saw a table with three bowls of porridge. She was really hungry from her long walk. First she tried the big bowl of porridge, but it was too hot. Then she tried the medium bowl of porridge, but it was too cold. She tried the little bowl of porridge, and it was just right. So she ate it all up.

1

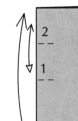

2

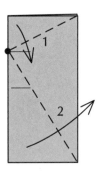

Fold and unfold to find the quarter mark.

3

4

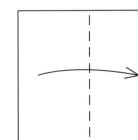

5

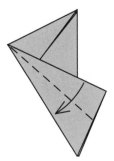

6

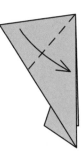

7

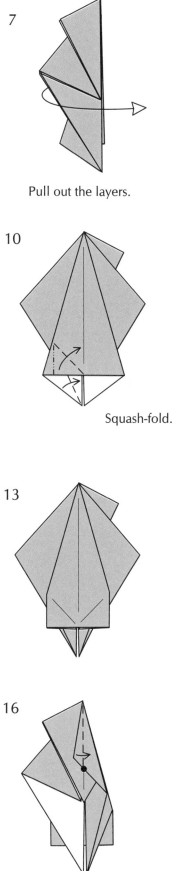

Pull out the layers.

8

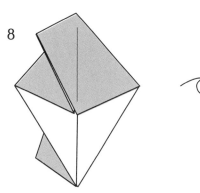

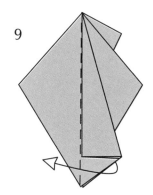

9

Pull out the layers.

10

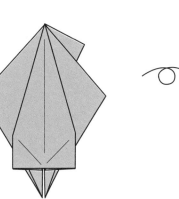

Squash-fold.

11

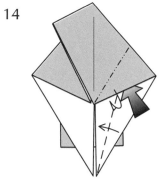

12

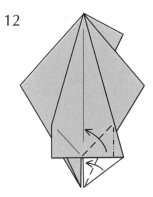

Repeat steps 10–11 on the right.

13

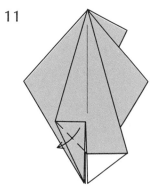

14

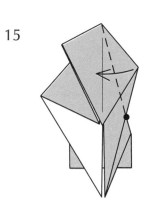

Unfold.

15

16

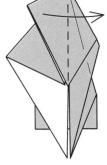

17

18

19

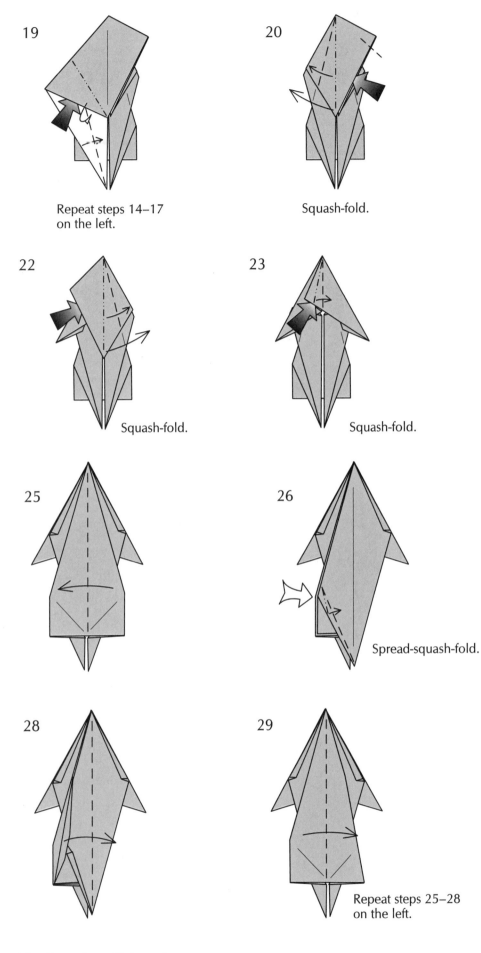

Repeat steps 14–17
on the left.

20

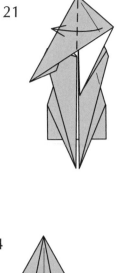

Squash-fold.

21

Squash-fold.

22

Squash-fold.

23

Squash-fold.

24

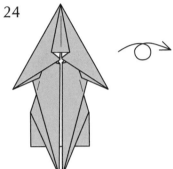

25

26

Spread-squash-fold.

27

28

29

Repeat steps 25–28
on the left.

30

Tuck inside.

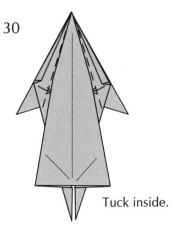
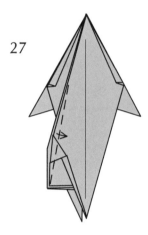

31

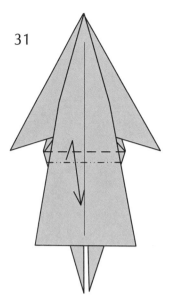

32

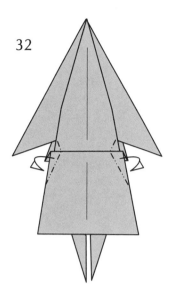

33

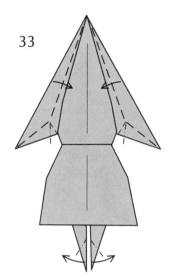

Rabbit-ear the arms and reverse-fold the feet.

34

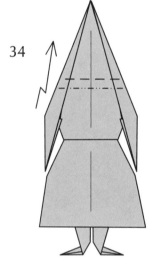

35

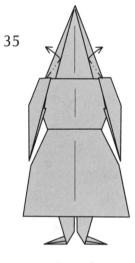

Spread.

36

37

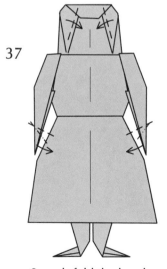

Squash-fold the hands.

38

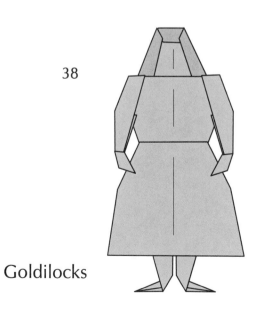

Goldilocks

Bear

Meanwhile, the bears were enjoying their walk in the deep forest.

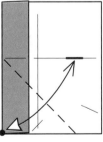

1
Fold and unfold.

2
Fold and unfold on the left.

3
Fold and unfold.

4
Fold and unfold at the bottom.

5

6
Fold and unfold.

7

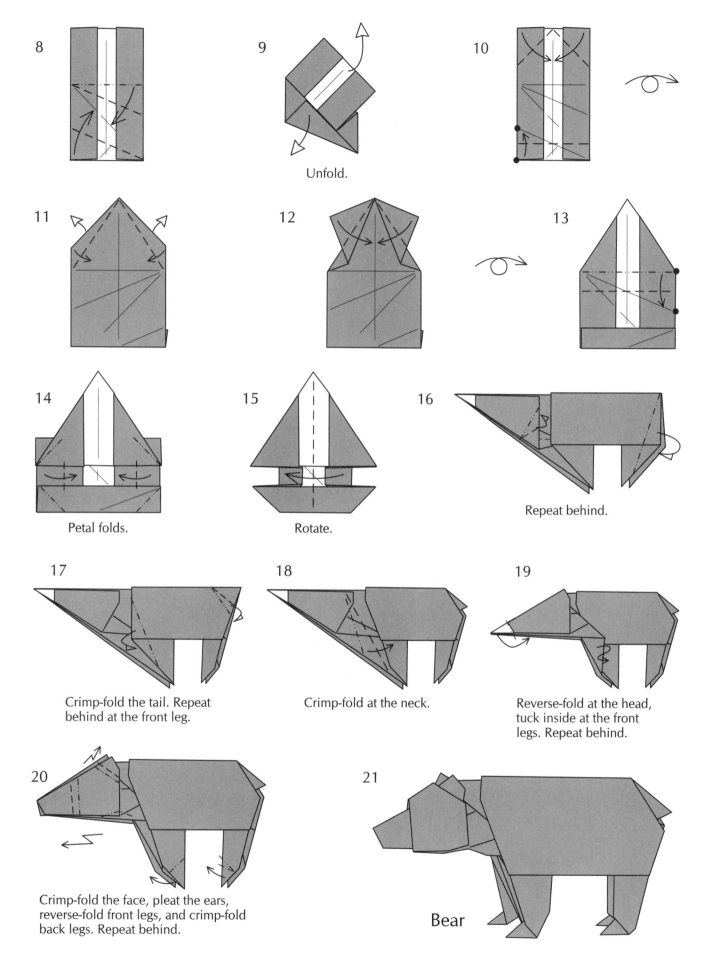

8

9

Unfold.

10

11

12

13

14

Petal folds.

15

Rotate.

16

Repeat behind.

17

Crimp-fold the tail. Repeat behind at the front leg.

18

Crimp-fold at the neck.

19

Reverse-fold at the head, tuck inside at the front legs. Repeat behind.

20

Crimp-fold the face, pleat the ears, reverse-fold front legs, and crimp-fold back legs. Repeat behind.

21

Bear

Flower

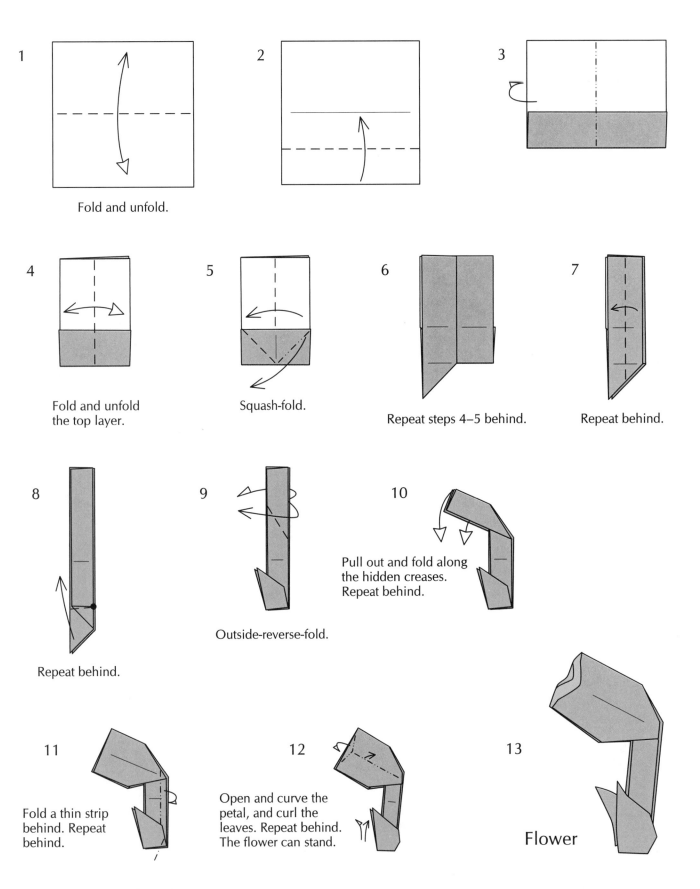

1

Fold and unfold.

2

3

4

Fold and unfold
the top layer.

5

Squash-fold.

6

Repeat steps 4–5 behind.

7

Repeat behind.

8

Repeat behind.

9

Outside-reverse-fold.

10

Pull out and fold along
the hidden creases.
Repeat behind.

11

Fold a thin strip
behind. Repeat
behind.

12

Open and curve the
petal, and curl the
leaves. Repeat behind.
The flower can stand.

13

Flower

Wide Tree

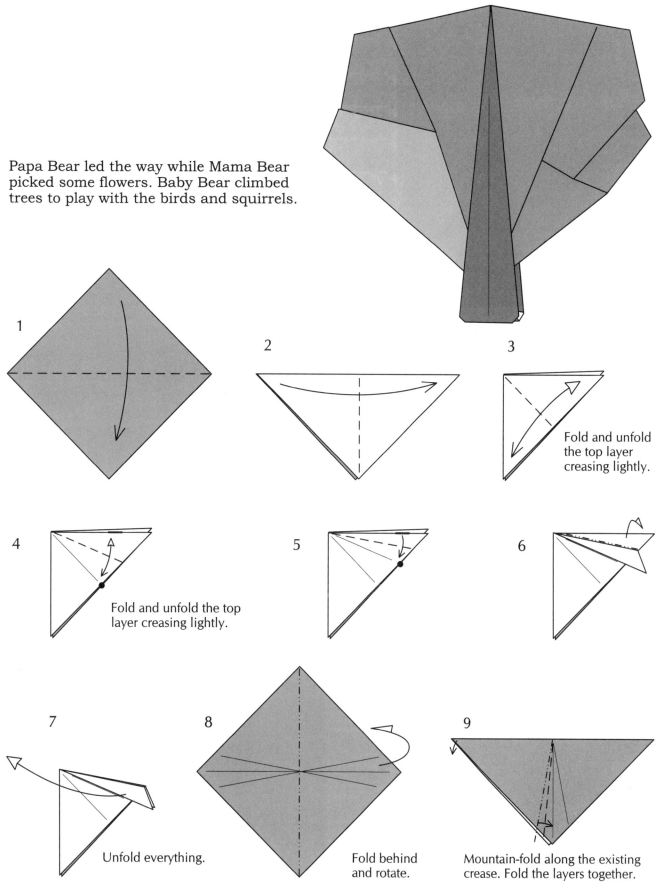

Papa Bear led the way while Mama Bear picked some flowers. Baby Bear climbed trees to play with the birds and squirrels.

1

2

3

Fold and unfold the top layer creasing lightly.

4

Fold and unfold the top layer creasing lightly.

5

6

7

8

Unfold everything.

Fold behind and rotate.

9

Mountain-fold along the existing crease. Fold the layers together.

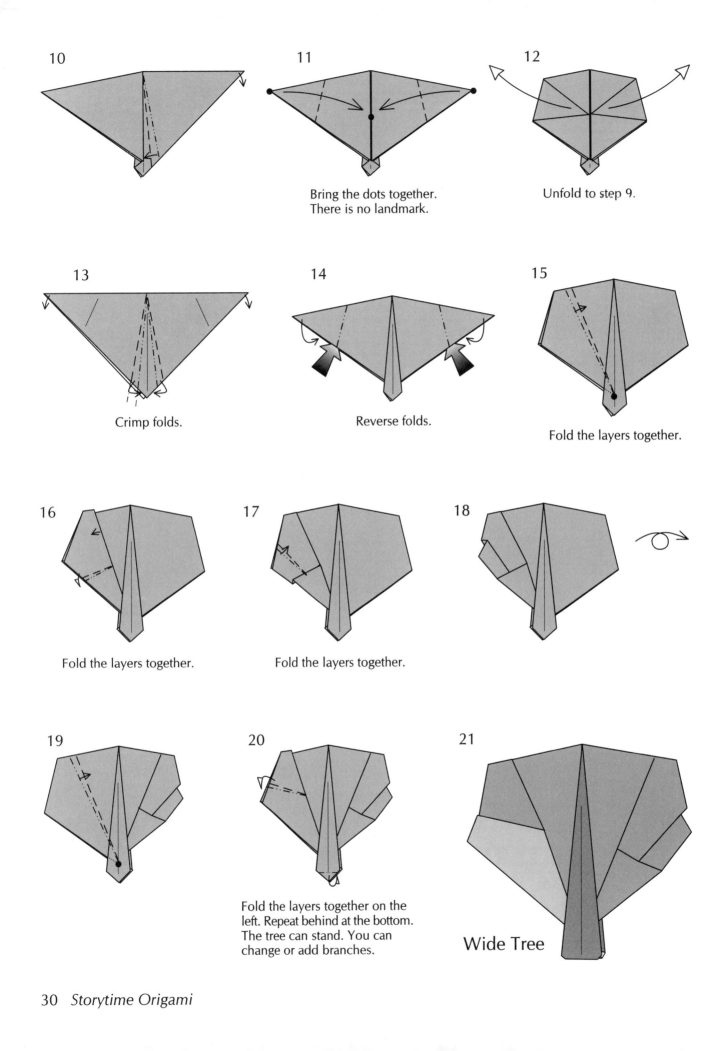

10

11

Bring the dots together.
There is no landmark.

12

Unfold to step 9.

13

Crimp folds.

14

Reverse folds.

15

Fold the layers together.

16

Fold the layers together.

17

Fold the layers together.

18

19

20

Fold the layers together on the
left. Repeat behind at the bottom.
The tree can stand. You can
change or add branches.

21

Wide Tree

Oval Tree

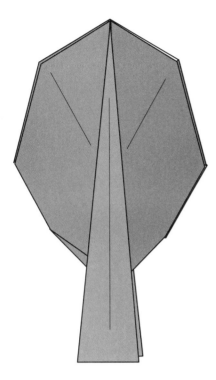

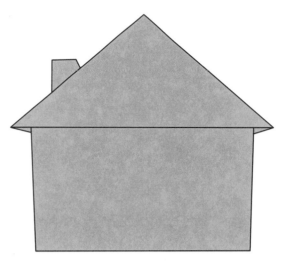

Back at the house, Goldilocks was getting tired so she went into the living room to sit on a chair.

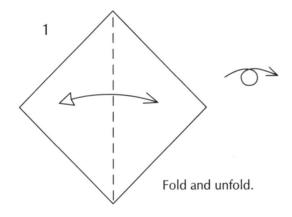

1

Fold and unfold.

2

3

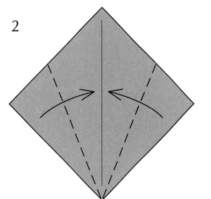

4

Unfold.

5

6

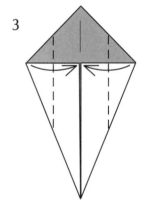

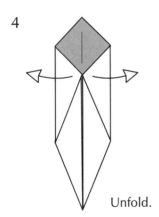

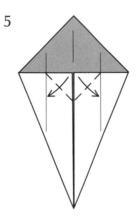

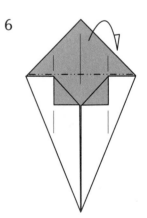

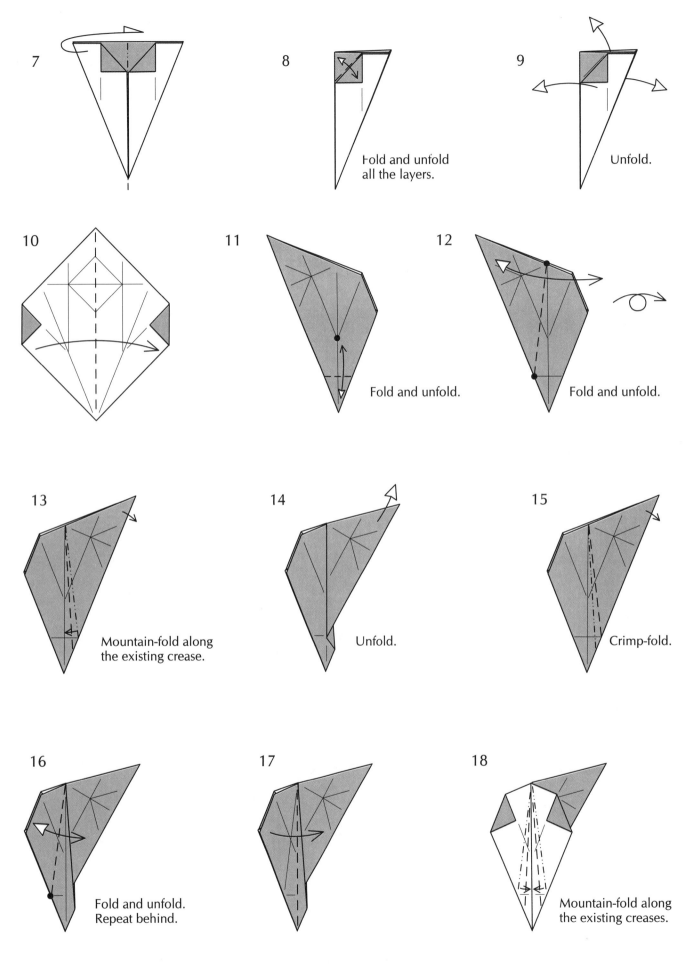

7

8 Fold and unfold all the layers.

9 Unfold.

10

11 Fold and unfold.

12 Fold and unfold.

13 Mountain-fold along the existing crease.

14 Unfold.

15 Crimp-fold.

16 Fold and unfold. Repeat behind.

17

18 Mountain-fold along the existing creases.

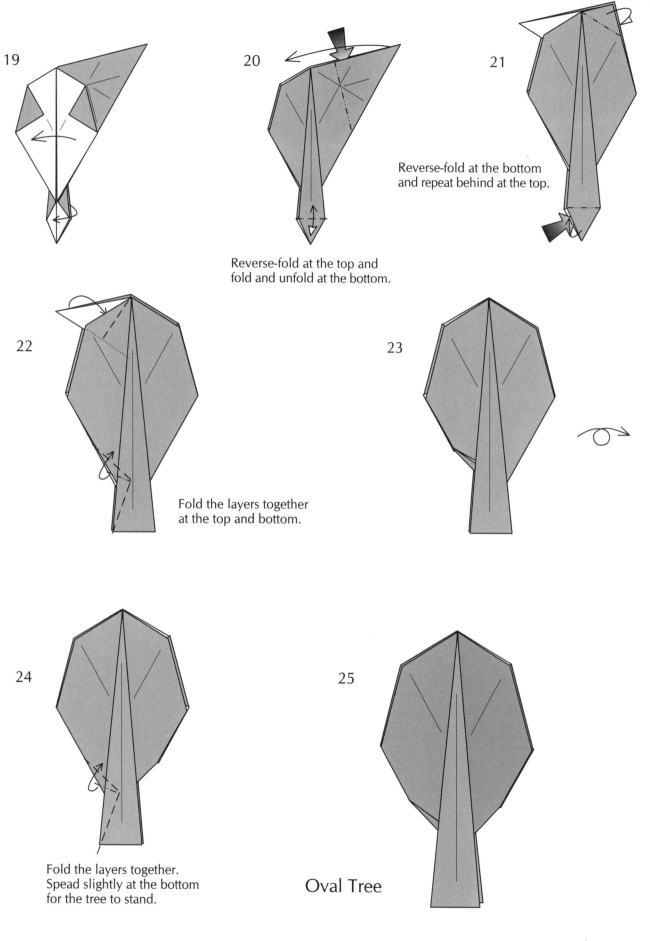

19

20

Reverse-fold at the top and
fold and unfold at the bottom.

21

Reverse-fold at the bottom
and repeat behind at the top.

22

Fold the layers together
at the top and bottom.

23

24

Fold the layers together.
Spead slightly at the bottom
for the tree to stand.

25

Oval Tree

Evergreen

First she sat on Papa Bear's chair, but it was too big. Then she sat on Mama Bear's chair, but it was also too big. So she tried Baby Bear's chair, and it was just right. But when she sat down, the chair broke apart.

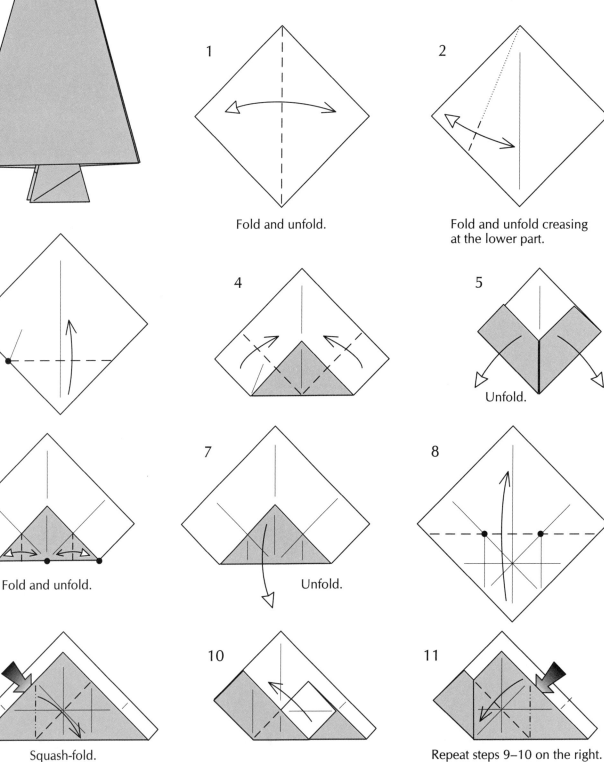

1

Fold and unfold.

2

Fold and unfold creasing at the lower part.

3

4

5

Unfold.

6

Fold and unfold.

7

Unfold.

8

9

Squash-fold.

10

11

Repeat steps 9–10 on the right.

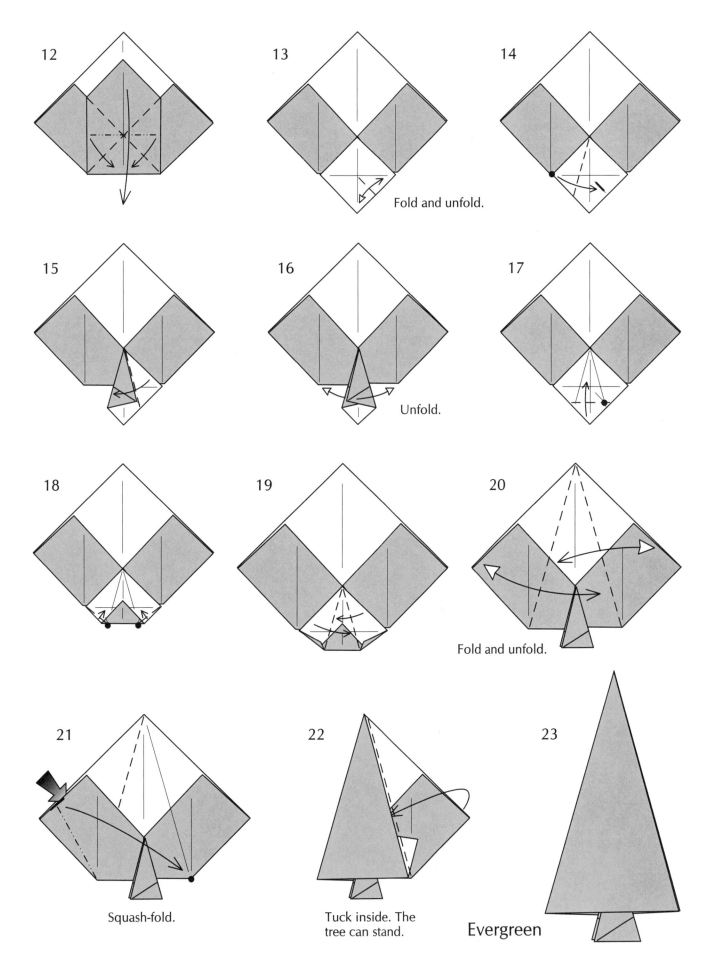

12

13

Fold and unfold.

14

15

16

Unfold.

17

18

19

20

Fold and unfold.

21

Squash-fold.

22

Tuck inside. The
tree can stand.

23

Evergreen

Squirrel

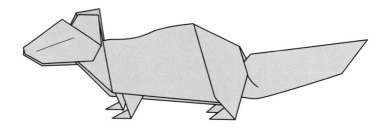

Goldilocks went upstairs to go to sleep. She lay on Papa Bear's bed, but it was too hard. She lay on Mama Bear's bed, but it was too soft. Then she lay on Baby Bear's bed, and it was just right, so she fell fast asleep.

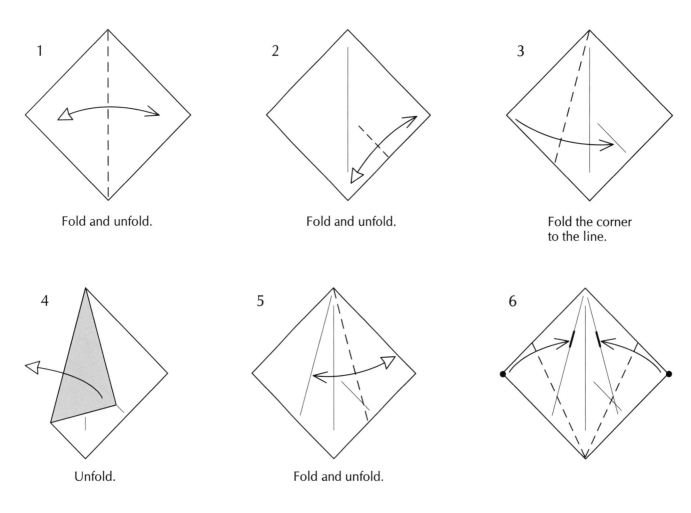

1

Fold and unfold.

2

Fold and unfold.

3

Fold the corner to the line.

4

Unfold.

5

Fold and unfold.

6

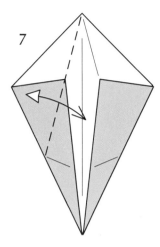

7

Fold and unfold.

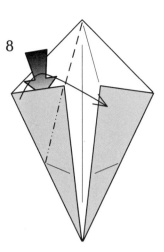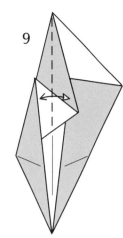

8

Reverse-fold.

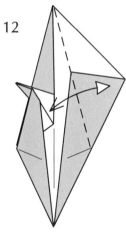

9

Fold and unfold.

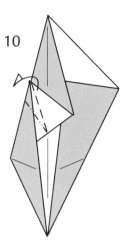

10

Squash-fold.

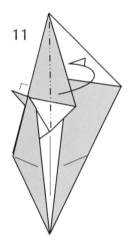

11

Note the right angle.

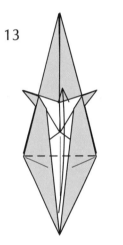

12

Repeat steps 7–11 on the right.

13

14

Spread the tail.

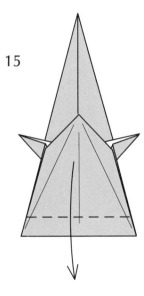

15

16

Squash folds.

17

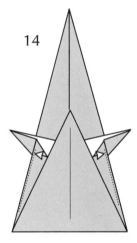

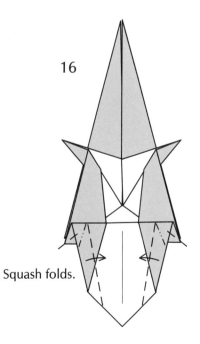

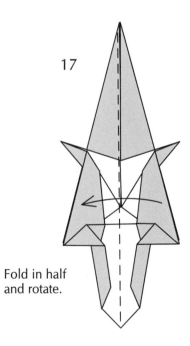

Fold in half and rotate.

Squirrel 37

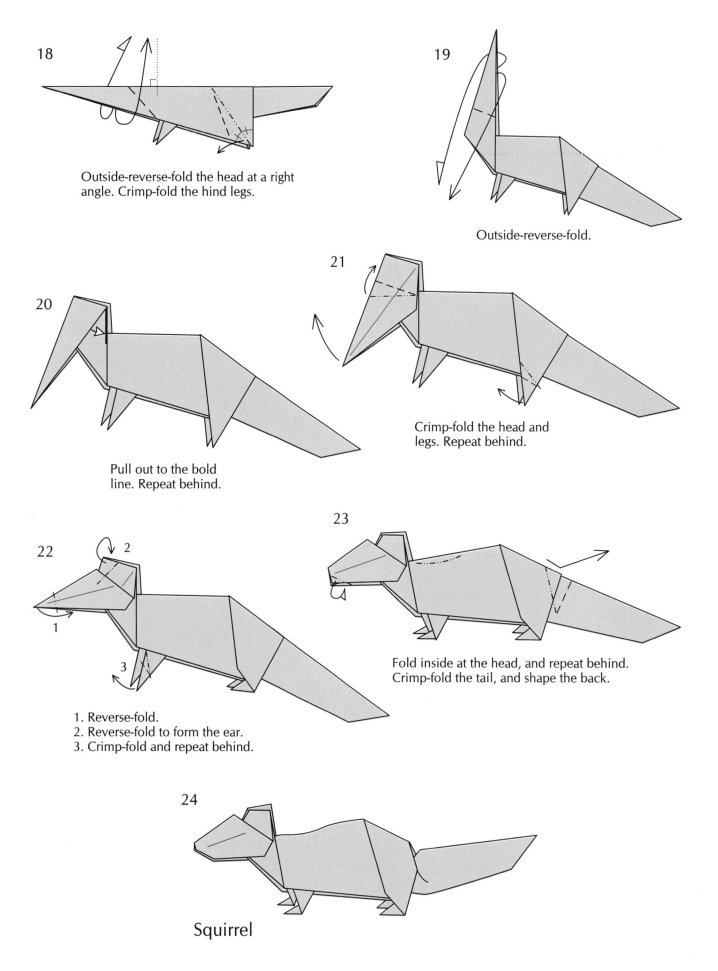

18 Outside-reverse-fold the head at a right angle. Crimp-fold the hind legs.

19 Outside-reverse-fold.

20 Pull out to the bold line. Repeat behind.

21 Crimp-fold the head and legs. Repeat behind.

22
1. Reverse-fold.
2. Reverse-fold to form the ear.
3. Crimp-fold and repeat behind.

23 Fold inside at the head, and repeat behind. Crimp-fold the tail, and shape the back.

24

Squirrel

House

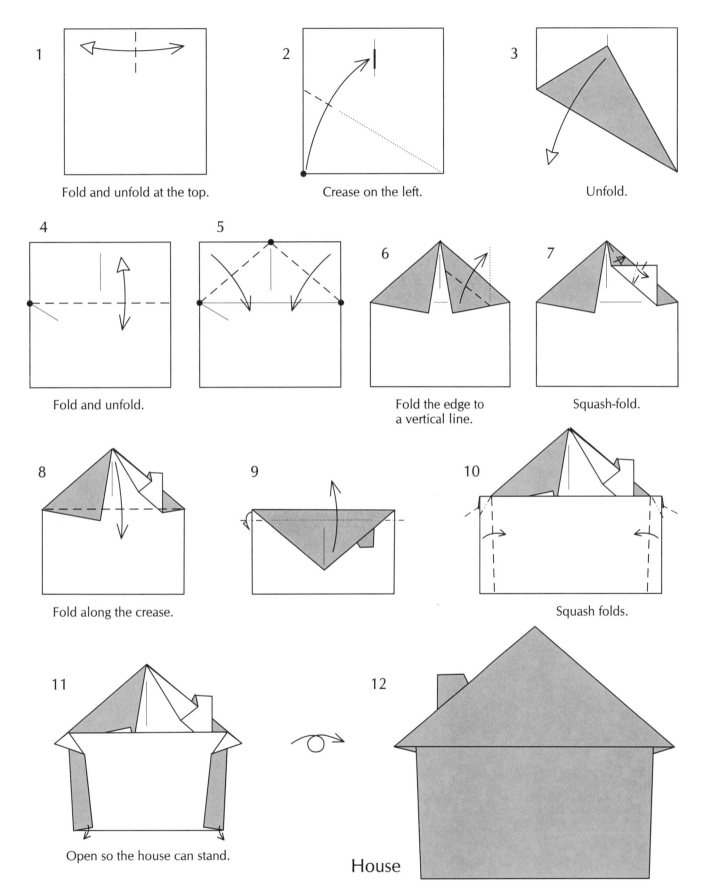

1 Fold and unfold at the top.

2 Crease on the left.

3 Unfold.

4 Fold and unfold.

5

6 Fold the edge to a vertical line.

7 Squash-fold.

8 Fold along the crease.

9

10 Squash folds.

11 Open so the house can stand.

12 House

Table

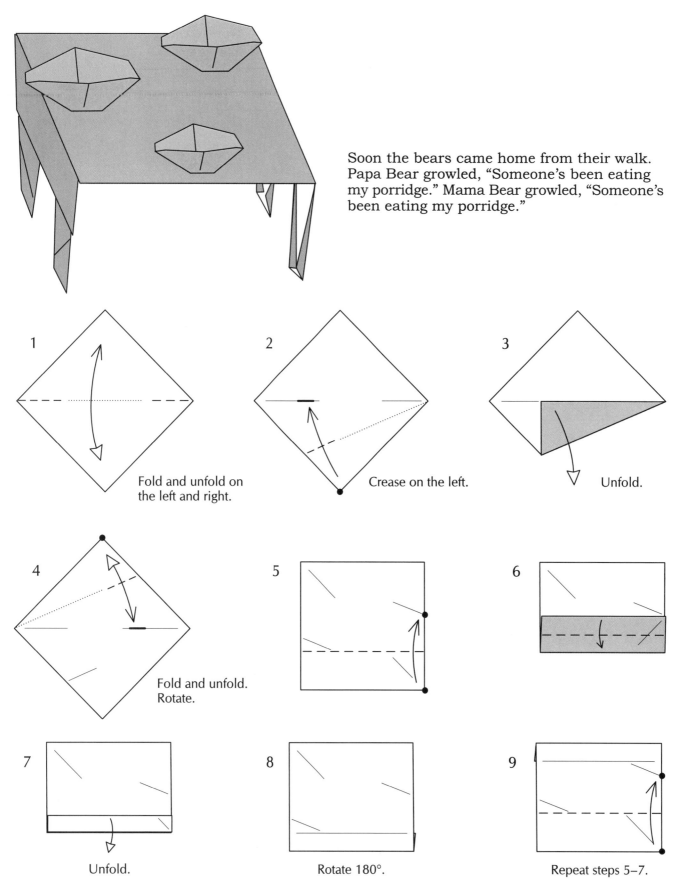

Soon the bears came home from their walk. Papa Bear growled, "Someone's been eating my porridge." Mama Bear growled, "Someone's been eating my porridge."

1

Fold and unfold on the left and right.

2

Crease on the left.

3

Unfold.

4

Fold and unfold. Rotate.

5

6

7

Unfold.

8

Rotate 180°.

9

Repeat steps 5–7.

10

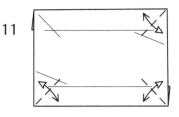

Fold and unfold
the top layer.

11

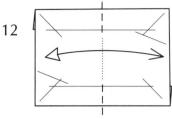

Fold and unfold
the top layer.

12

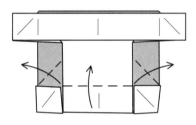

Fold in half and unfold creasing
at the top and bottom.

13

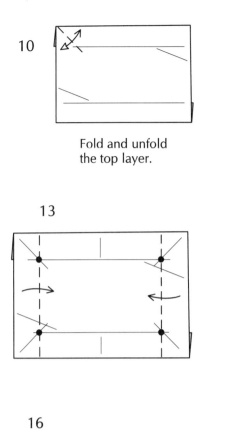

14

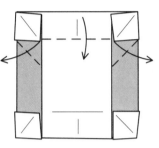

Petal-fold.

15

Petal-fold.

16

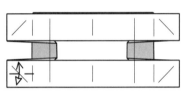

Fold and unfold.

17

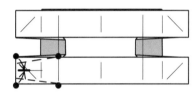

Fold and unfold the top layer.

18

Fold the left corners to the center
crease. Fold all layers at the bottom.

19

Repeat steps 17–18
three more times.

20

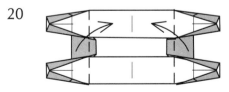

Fold along the crease towards
the center. Turn over.

21

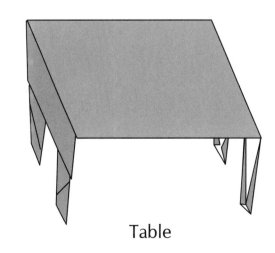

Table

Table 41

Bowl

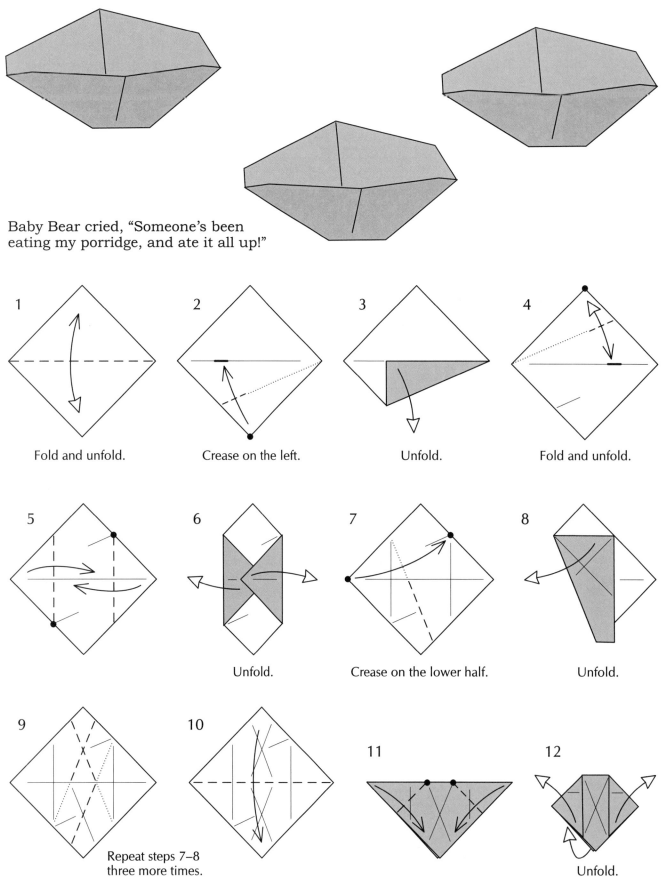

Baby Bear cried, "Someone's been eating my porridge, and ate it all up!"

1 Fold and unfold.

2 Crease on the left.

3 Unfold.

4 Fold and unfold.

5

6 Unfold.

7 Crease on the lower half.

8 Unfold.

9 Repeat steps 7–8 three more times.

10

11

12 Unfold.

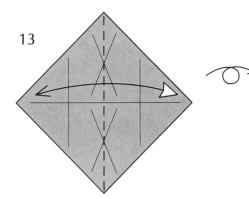

13

Fold and unfold.

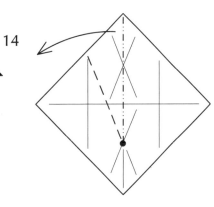

14

Push in at the dot.

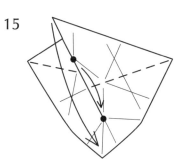

15

The model is 3D.

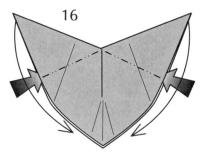

16

Reverse folds along the creases.

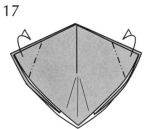

17

Fold inside along the creases and repeat behind.

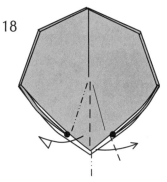

18

The dots indicate the corners of the inner layers. Fold above the dot on the left and below the dot on the right.

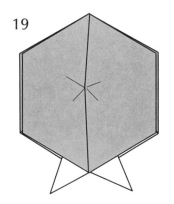

19

The bowl is 3D and goes down in the center.

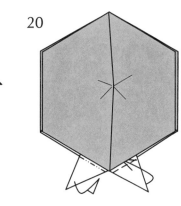

20

The bottom of the bowl resembles a hill. Tuck inside wrapping around hidden layers.

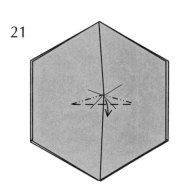

21

Flatten in the center.

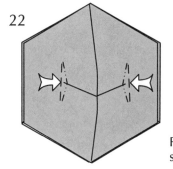

22

Push in to shape the bottom so the sides are curved.

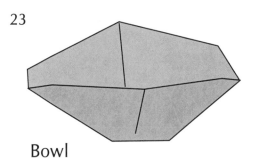

23

Bowl

Chair

The bears went to the living room. Papa Bear growled, "Someone's been sitting on my chair." Mama Bear growled, "Someone's been sitting on my chair." Baby Bear cried, "Someone's been sitting on my chair, and broke it all up!"

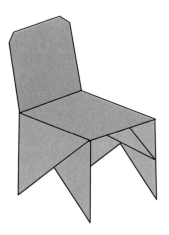

1

Fold and unfold.

2

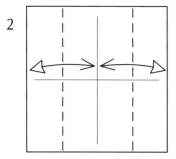

Fold and unfold.

3

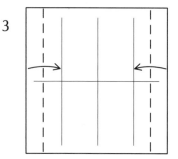

4

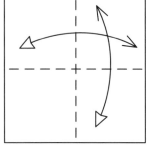

5

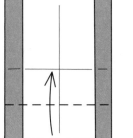

Squash-fold.

6

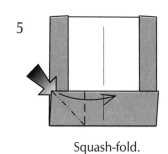

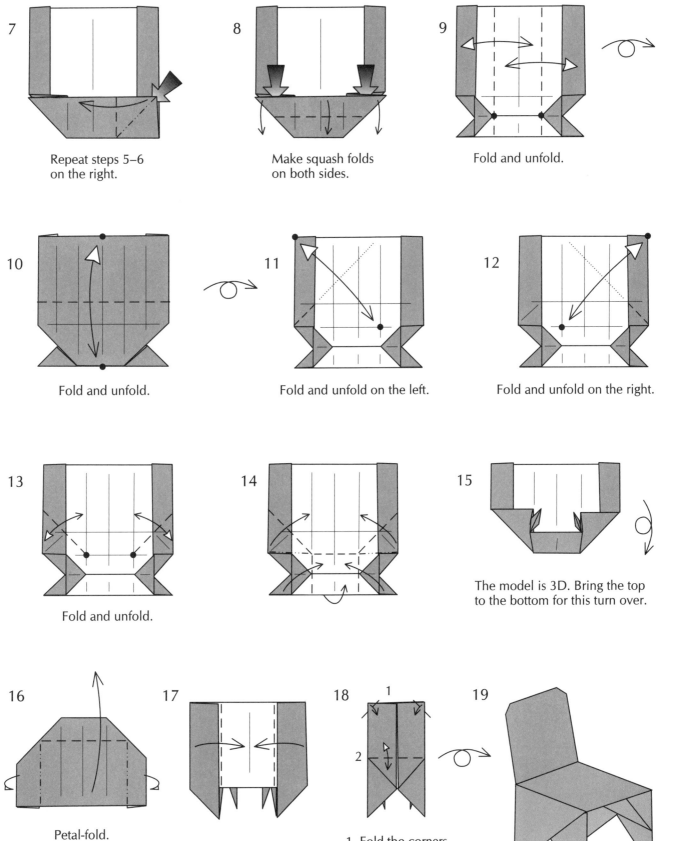

7 Repeat steps 5–6 on the right.

8 Make squash folds on both sides.

9 Fold and unfold.

10 Fold and unfold.

11 Fold and unfold on the left.

12 Fold and unfold on the right.

13 Fold and unfold.

14

15 The model is 3D. Bring the top to the bottom for this turn over.

16 Petal-fold.

17

18
1. Fold the corners.
2. Fold and unfold.

19

Chair

Bed

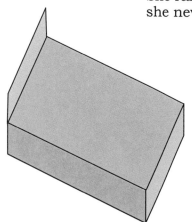

They went upstairs. Papa Bear growled, "Someone's been sleeping in my bed." Mama Bear growled, "Someone's been sleeping in my bed." Baby Bear cried, "Someone's been sleeping in my bed, and there she is!" All of a sudden Goldilocks woke up. She saw the three bears and jumped out of bed. She ran, and ran, and ran until she was home, and she never wandered into the woods again.

1

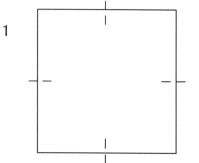

Fold by the edges and unfold.

2

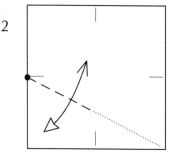

Fold and unfold.

3

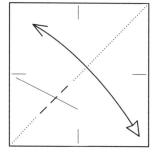

Fold and unfold creasing on the previous crease.

4

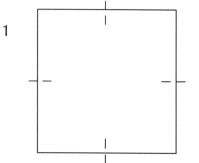

5

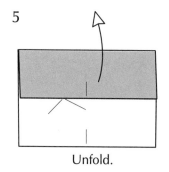

Unfold.

6

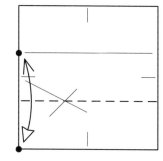

Fold and unfold.

7

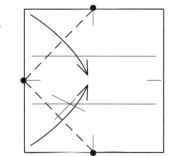

8

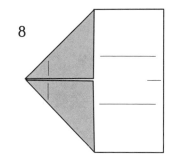

9

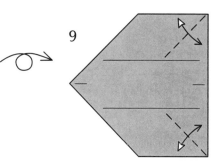

Fold and unfold.

10

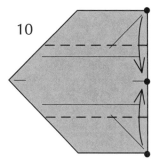

11

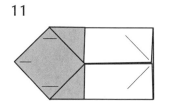

12

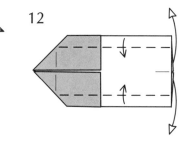

13

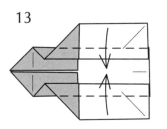

14

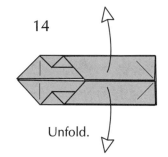

Unfold.

15

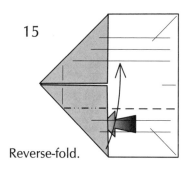

Reverse-fold.

16

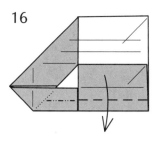

Reverse-fold.

17

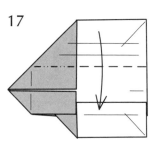

Repeat steps
15–16 at the top.

18

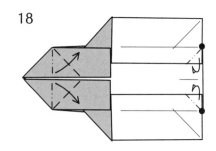

Petal-fold on the left.

Bed 47

19

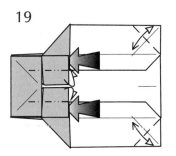

Tuck into the middle
layer on the left. Fold
and unfold on the right.

20

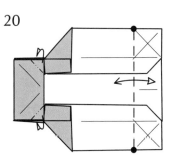

Fold and unfold on the right.

21

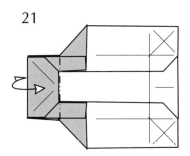

Fold and unfold.

22

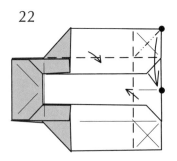

23

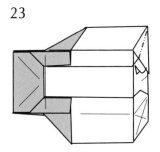

The model is 3D. Tuck inside.

24

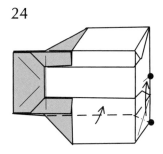

Repeat steps 22–24.

25

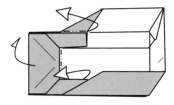

Pull out and turn over.

26

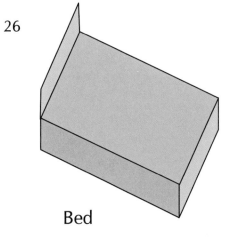

Bed

The Three Little Pigs

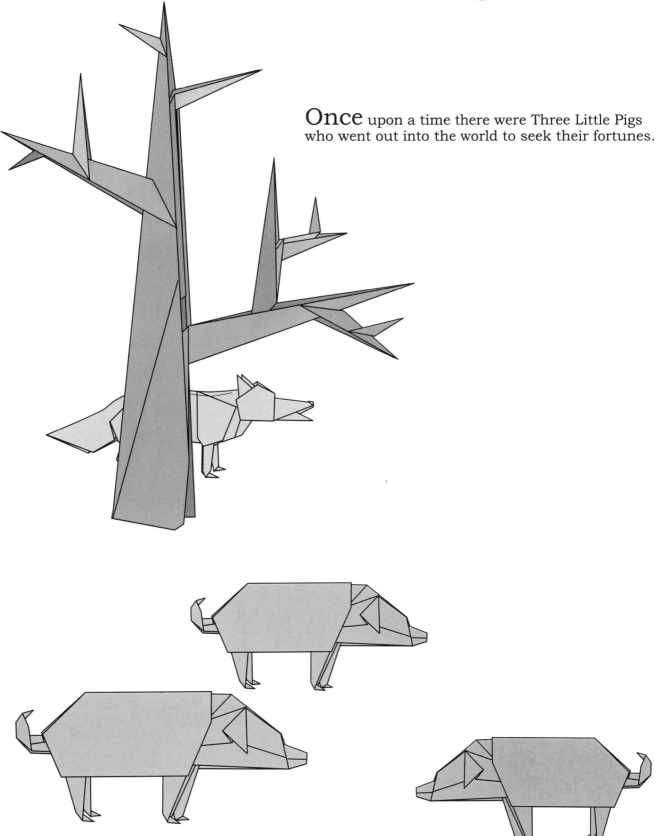

Once upon a time there were Three Little Pigs who went out into the world to seek their fortunes.

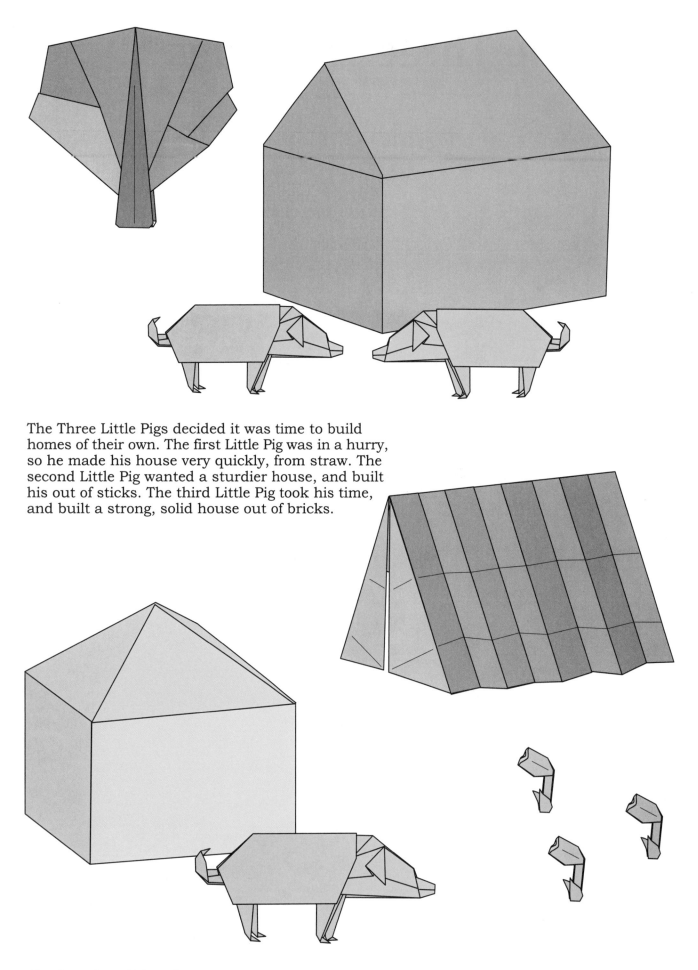

The Three Little Pigs decided it was time to build
homes of their own. The first Little Pig was in a hurry,
so he made his house very quickly, from straw. The
second Little Pig wanted a sturdier house, and built
his out of sticks. The third Little Pig took his time,
and built a strong, solid house out of bricks.

Pig

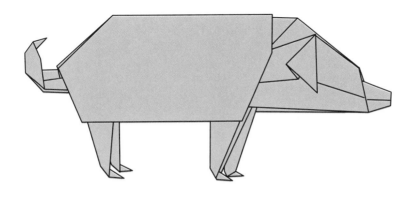

The Three Little Pigs were living happily in
the houses they had built for themselves,
but trouble was just around the corner.

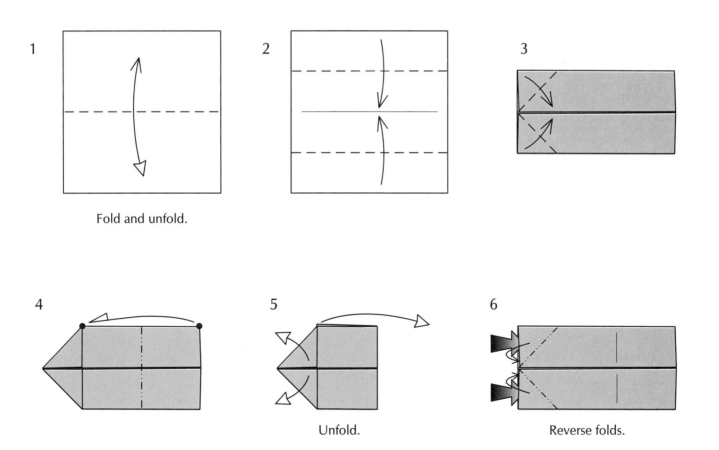

1

Fold and unfold.

2

3

4

5

Unfold.

6

Reverse folds.

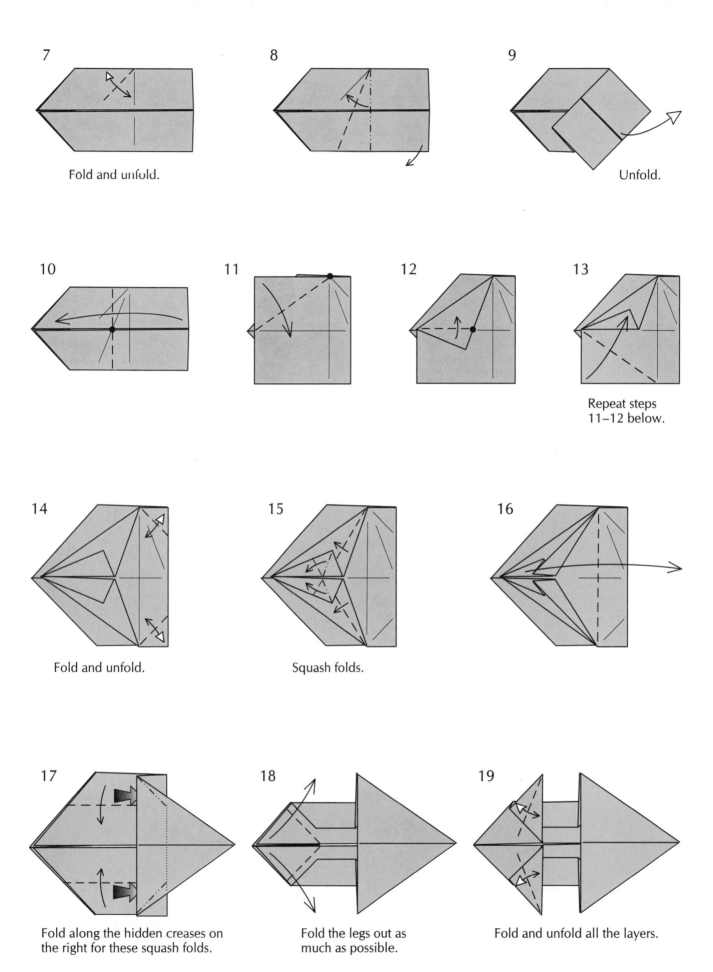

7

Fold and unfold.

8

9

Unfold.

10

11

12

13

Repeat steps
11–12 below.

14

Fold and unfold.

15

Squash folds.

16

17

Fold along the hidden creases on
the right for these squash folds.

18

Fold the legs out as
much as possible.

19

Fold and unfold all the layers.

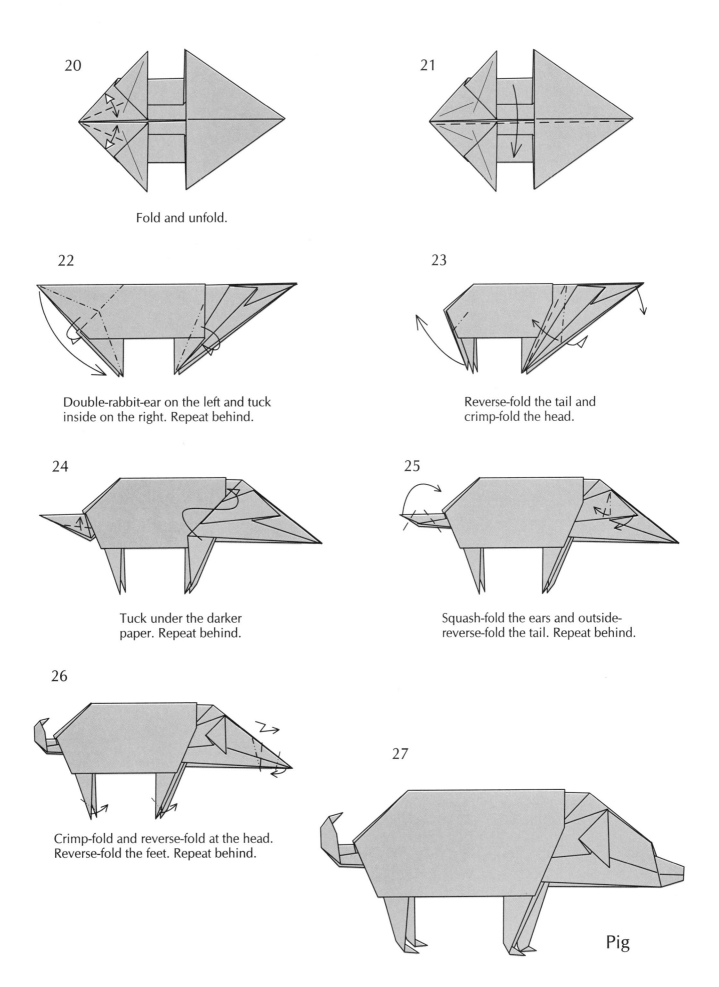

20

Fold and unfold.

21

22

Double-rabbit-ear on the left and tuck inside on the right. Repeat behind.

23

Reverse-fold the tail and crimp-fold the head.

24

Tuck under the darker paper. Repeat behind.

25

Squash-fold the ears and outside-reverse-fold the tail. Repeat behind.

26

Crimp-fold and reverse-fold at the head. Reverse-fold the feet. Repeat behind.

27

Pig

Wolf

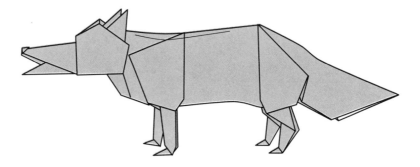

When they built their houses, they didn't know that their neighbor was the Big Bad Wolf. The Big Bad Wolf's favorite meal happened to be roast pig.

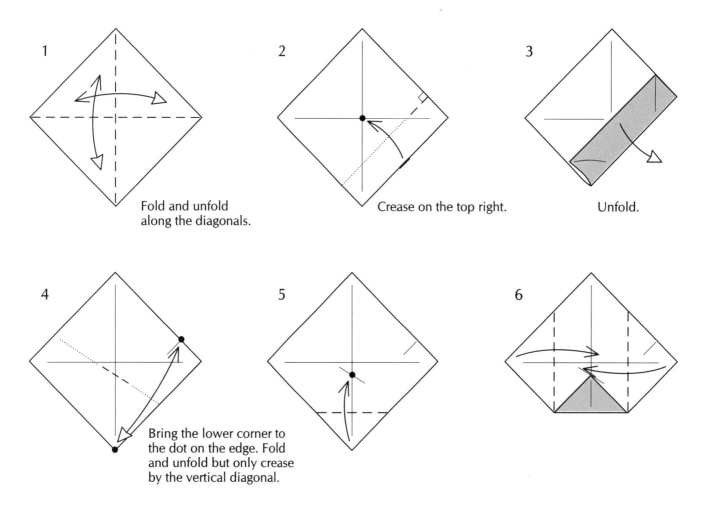

1

Fold and unfold
along the diagonals.

2

Crease on the top right.

3

Unfold.

4

Bring the lower corner to
the dot on the edge. Fold
and unfold but only crease
by the vertical diagonal.

5

6

7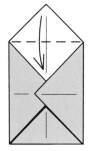

8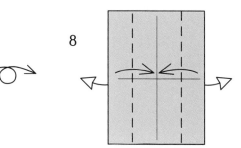

9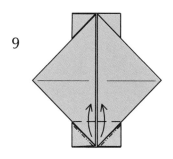

Squash folds.

10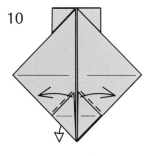

Spread.

11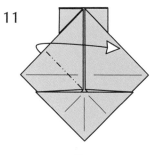

Pull out.

12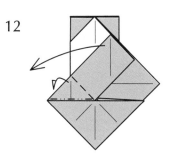

Refold back to step 11.

13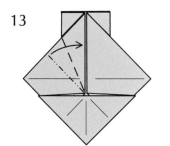

Mountain-fold along the crease.

14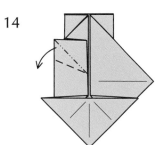

Mountain-fold along the
crease for this squash fold.

15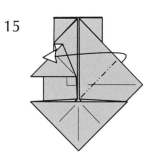

Note the right angle. Repeat
steps 11–14 on the right.

16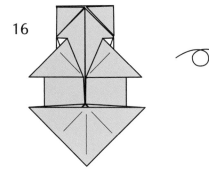

17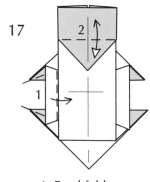

1. Petal-fold.
2. Fold and unfold.

18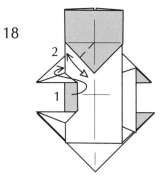

1. Tuck inside.
2. Fold and unfold.

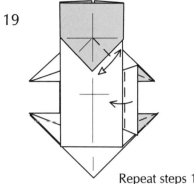

19

Repeat steps 17–18
on the right.

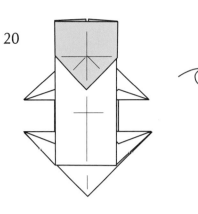

20

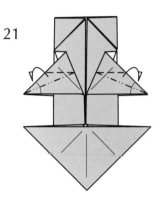

21

Bisect the angles.

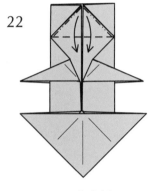

22

Squash folds.

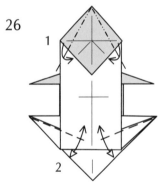

23

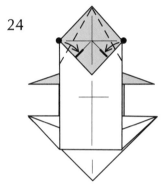

24

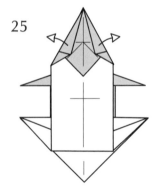

25

Unfold.

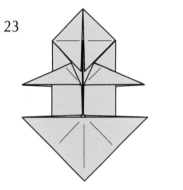

26

1

2

1. Reverse folds.
2. Fold and unfold
all the layers.

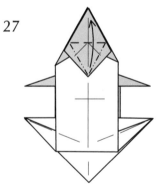

27

Petal-fold.

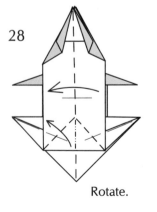

28

Rotate.

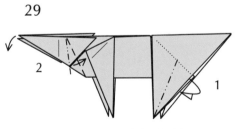

29

2

1

1. Mountain-fold the hidden
layer and repeat behind.
2. Crimp-fold.

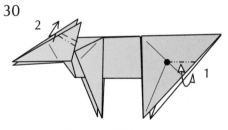

30

2

1

1. Fold and unfold.
2. Mountain and valley-fold all
the layers. Do not reverse fold.
Repeat behind.

31

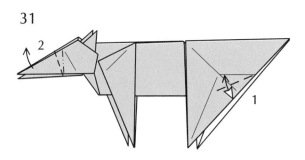

1. Fold and unfold. Repeat behind.
2. Crimp-fold.

32

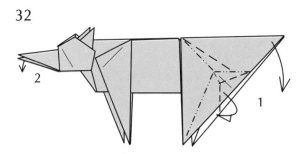

1. Shape the tail. This is similar to a crimp fold.
2. Separate the lower jaw.

33

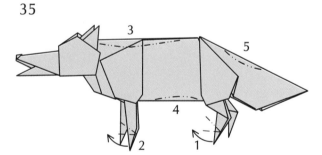

1. Double-rabbit-ear the hind legs. This is similar to a crimp fold.
2. Crimp-fold the front legs.
3. Outside-reverse-fold the nose.

34

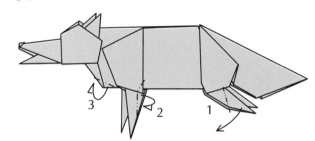

1. Reverse-fold.
2. Fold inside and repeat behind on the same leg.
3. Mountain-fold the neck. Repeat behind.

35

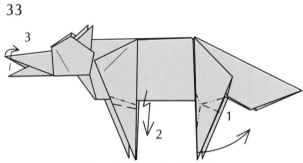

Crimp-fold the feet.
Shape the body and tail.

36

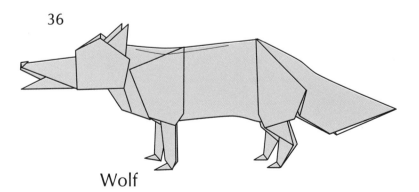

Wolf

Bare Tree

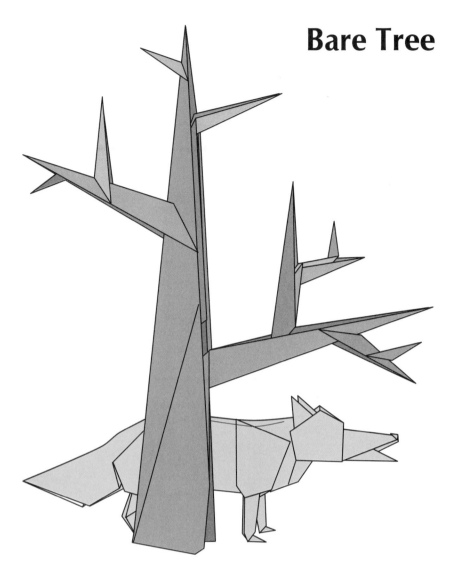

One day, the Big Bad Wolf got very hungry and went searching for his favorite meal.

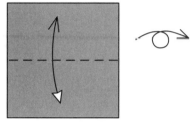

1 Fold and unfold.

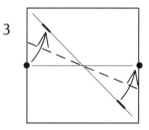

2 Fold and unfold.

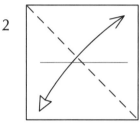

3 Fold to the landmarks and turn over to check on the back.

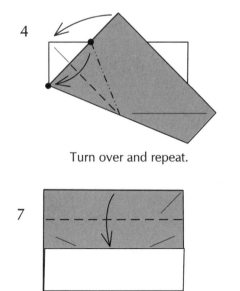

4 Turn over and repeat.

5 Unfold.

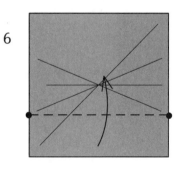

6

7

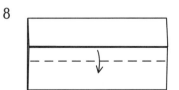

8 Fold along a hidden crease.

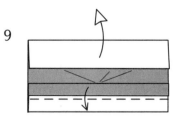

9 Unfold at the top.

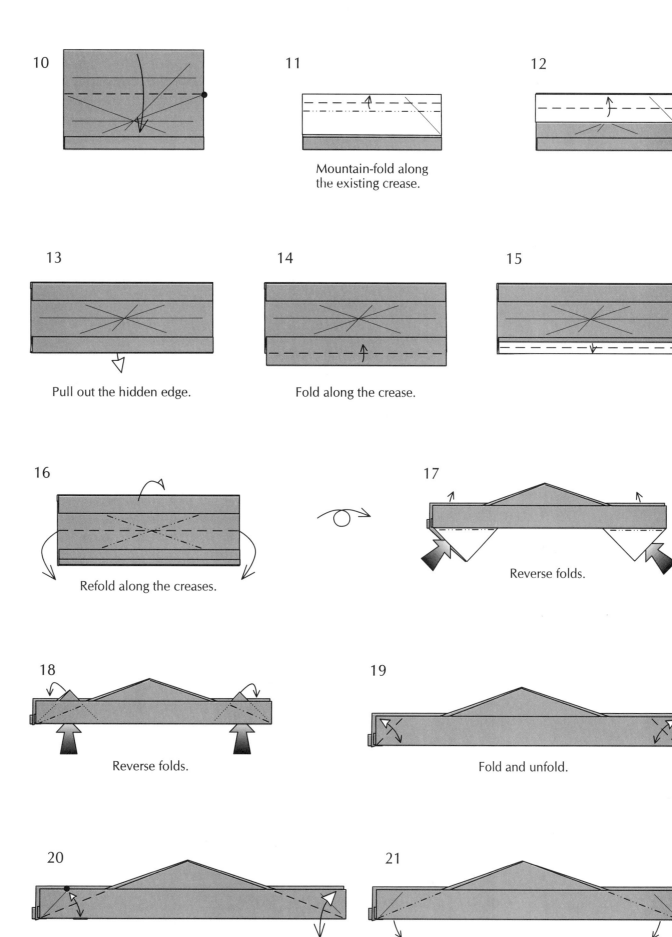

10

11

Mountain-fold along
the existing crease.

12

13

Pull out the hidden edge.

14

Fold along the crease.

15

16

Refold along the creases.

17

Reverse folds.

18

Reverse folds.

19

Fold and unfold.

20

Fold and unfold.

21

Reverse folds.

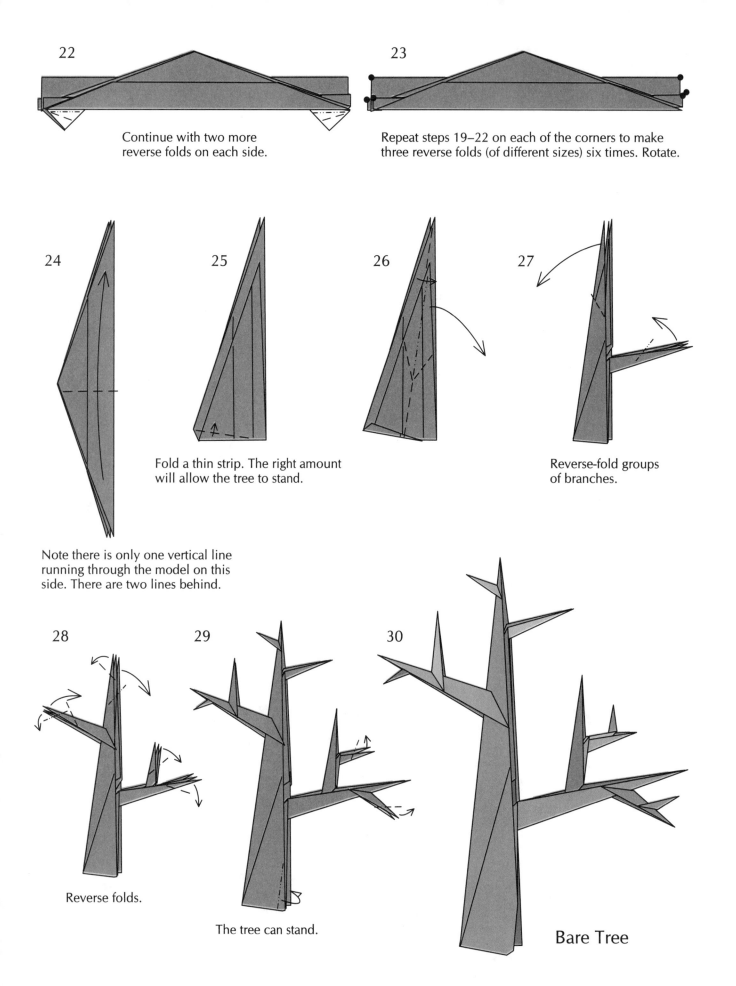

22

Continue with two more
reverse folds on each side.

23

Repeat steps 19–22 on each of the corners to make
three reverse folds (of different sizes) six times. Rotate.

24

25

Fold a thin strip. The right amount
will allow the tree to stand.

26

27

Reverse-fold groups
of branches.

Note there is only one vertical line
running through the model on this
side. There are two lines behind.

28

Reverse folds.

29

The tree can stand.

30

Bare Tree

Straw House

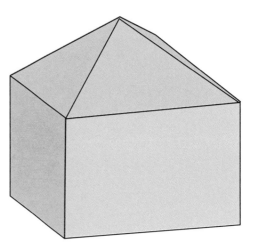

He came to the straw house of the first Little Pig and knocked on the door. "Little Pig, Little Pig, let me come in!" cried the Big Bad Wolf. "Not by the hair of my chinny-chin-chin!" answered the first Little Pig. "Then I'll huff and I'll puff and I'll blow your house in!" said the Big Bad Wolf, and he did. The first Little pig was fast, though, and ran to the house of his brother, the second Little Pig, before the Big Bad Wolf could catch him.

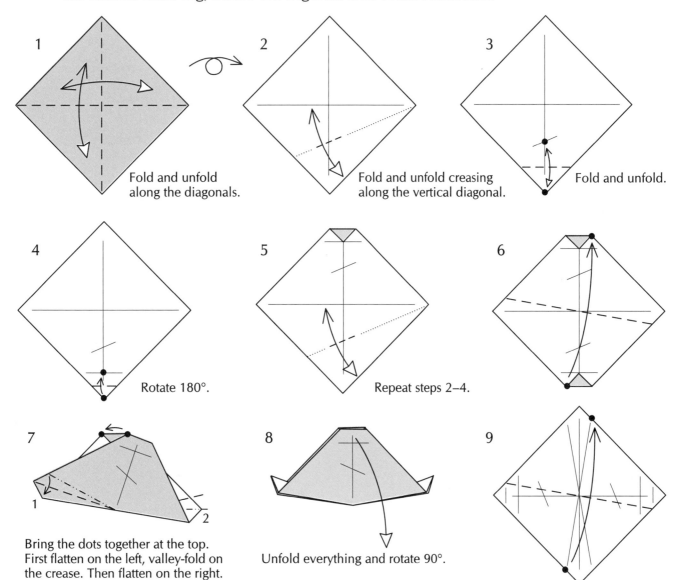

1

Fold and unfold along the diagonals.

2

Fold and unfold creasing along the vertical diagonal.

3

Fold and unfold.

4

Rotate 180°.

5

Repeat steps 2–4.

6

7

Bring the dots together at the top. First flatten on the left, valley-fold on the crease. Then flatten on the right.

8

Unfold everything and rotate 90°.

9

10

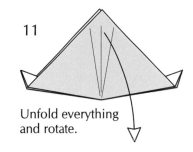

11

Unfold everything and rotate.

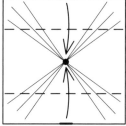

12

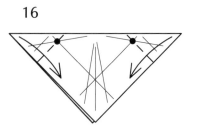

13

Unfold.

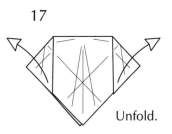

14

Fold and unfold.

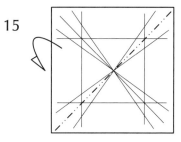

15

Rotate.

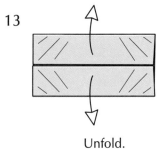

16

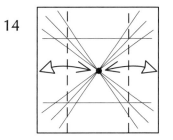

17

Unfold.

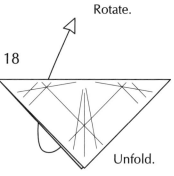

18

Unfold.

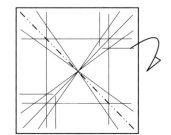

19

Repeat steps 15–18 in the other direction.

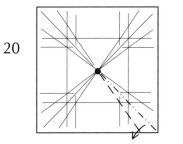

20

Push in at the dot.

21

The model is 3D. Push in at the upper dot.

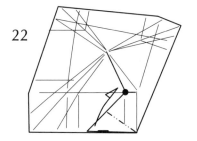

22

Bring the bold edge to the dot.

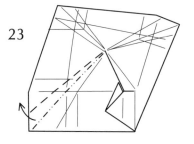

23

Repeat steps 20–23 three more times. Rotate.

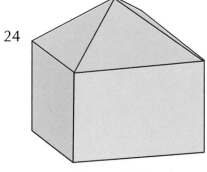

24

Straw House

Stick House

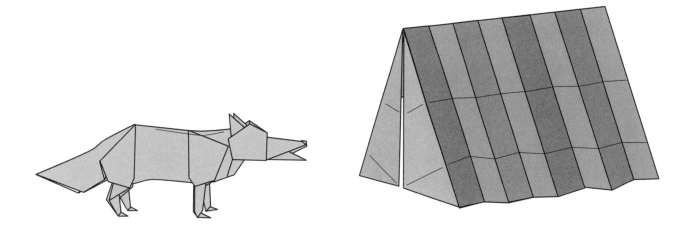

The Big Bad Wolf went to the house of sticks of the second Little Pig, and knocked on the door. "Little Pig, Little Pig, let me come in!" cried the Big Bad Wolf. "Not by the hair of my chinny-chin-chin!" answered the second Little Pig. "Then I'll huff and I'll puff and I'll blow your house in!" said the Big Bad Wolf, and again, he did. The first and second Little Pigs were fast, and ran to the house of their brother, the third Little Pig, narrowly escaping the clutches of the Big Bad Wolf.

1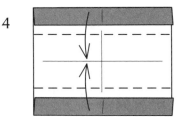

Fold and unfold.

2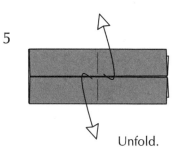

Fold and unfold creasing at the edges.

3

4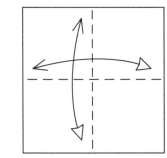

Fold to the center.

5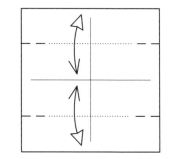

Unfold.

6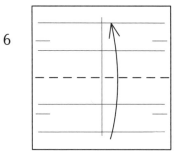

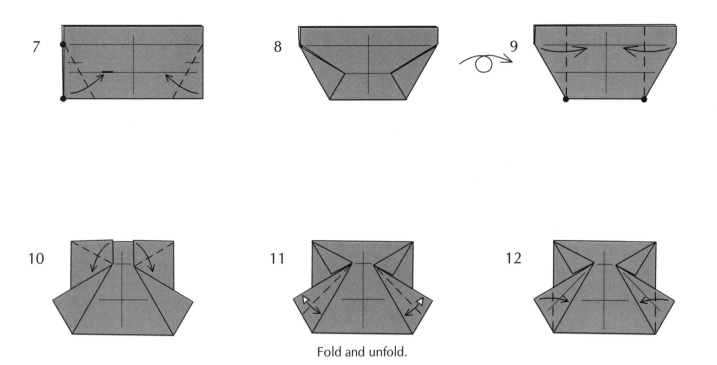

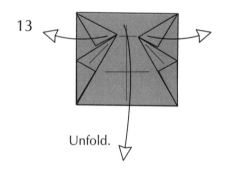

11

Fold and unfold.

12

13

Unfold.

14

Fold along the creases
and unfold. Rotate 90°.

15

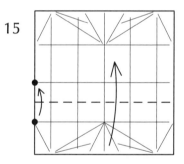

16

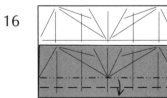

Mountain-fold the top
layer along the crease.

17

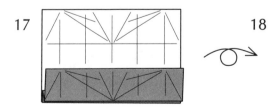

18

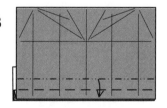

Mountain-fold the top
layer along the crease.

19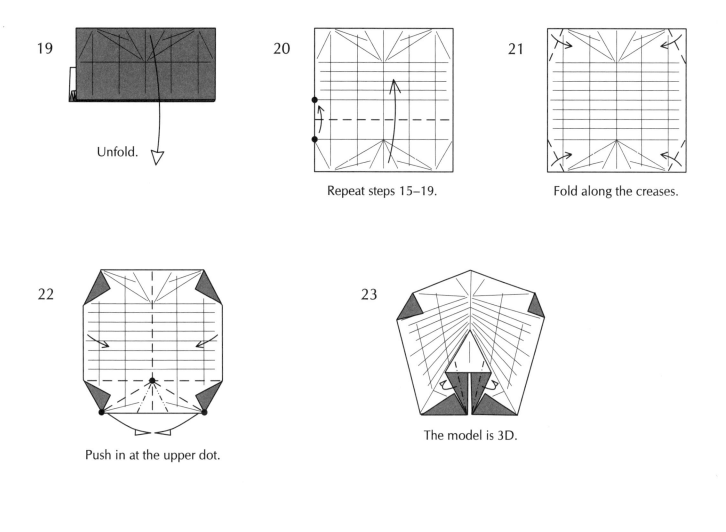

Unfold.

20

Repeat steps 15–19.

21

Fold along the creases.

22

Push in at the upper dot.

23

The model is 3D.

24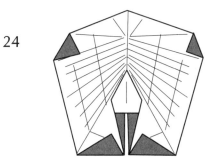

Repeat steps 22–23 on the other side. Rotate.

25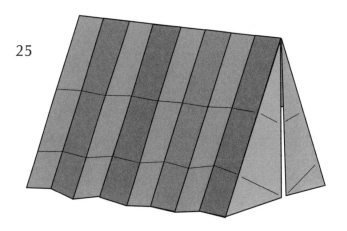

Stick House

Brick House

The Big Bad Wolf came to the brick house of the third Little Pig, and knocked on the door. "Little Pig, Little Pig, let me come in!" cried the Big Bad Wolf. "Not by the hair of my chinny-chin-chin!" answered the third Little Pig. "Then I'll huff and I'll puff and I'll blow your house in!" said the Big Bad Wolf. The Big Bad Wolf began to huff and puff, but the house didn't fall down. He huffed and puffed even harder, and still the brick house stood strong. He was getting tired from all of the huffing and puffing and realized that he would have to find another way to catch those Three Little Pigs. So he yelled angrily, "If you won't let me in through the door, I'm going to come down the chimney!"

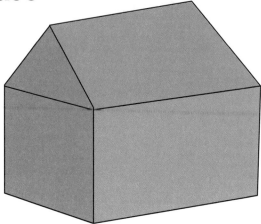

When the third Little Pig inside the brick house heard the Big Bad Wolf say he was going to come down the chimney, he had a clever idea. He put a big pot of boiling water over the fire. The Big Bad Wolf started to climb down the chimney but his tail went into the boiling water. He yelped and scurried as fast as he could up and out of the chimney and ran and ran and ran, and the Big Bad Wolf was never seen or heard from again.

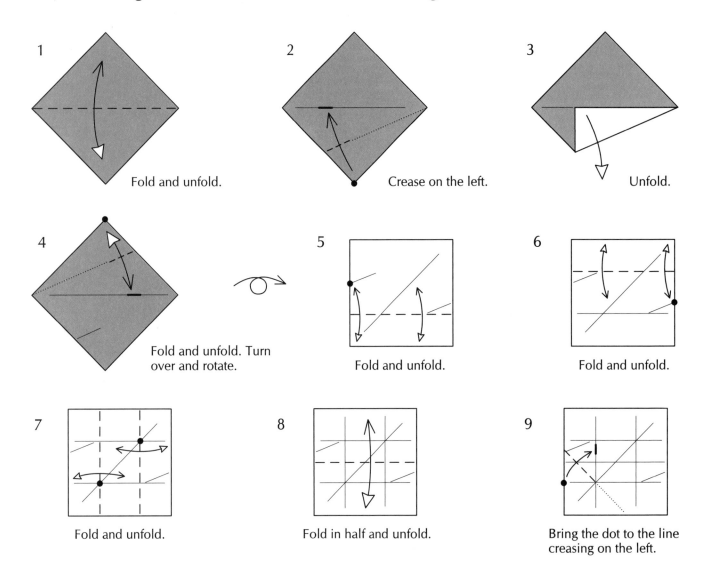

1. Fold and unfold.

2. Crease on the left.

3. Unfold.

4. Fold and unfold. Turn over and rotate.

5. Fold and unfold.

6. Fold and unfold.

7. Fold and unfold.

8. Fold in half and unfold.

9. Bring the dot to the line creasing on the left.

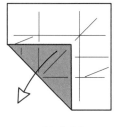

10

Unfold.

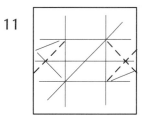

11

Fold and unfold
three more times.

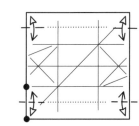

12

Fold and unfold by the edges.

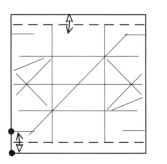

13

Fold and unfold.

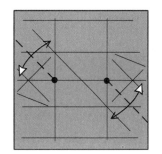

14

Fold and unfold.

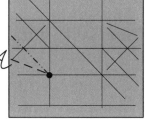

15

Puff out at the dot as
the model becomes 3D.

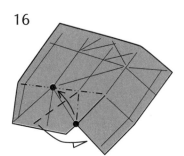

16

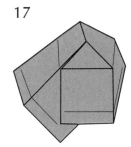

17

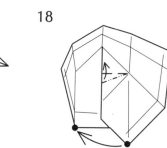

18

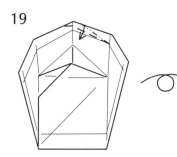

19

Repeat steps 15–18 and
rotate to view the outside

20

Wrap all around.

21

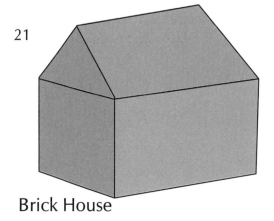

Brick House

Humpty Dumpty

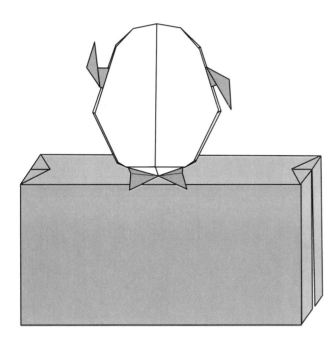

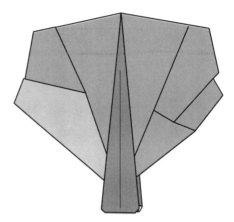

Humpty Dumpty sat on a wall.
Humpty Dumpty had a great fall.
All the king's horses and all the king's men
Couldn't put Humpty together again!

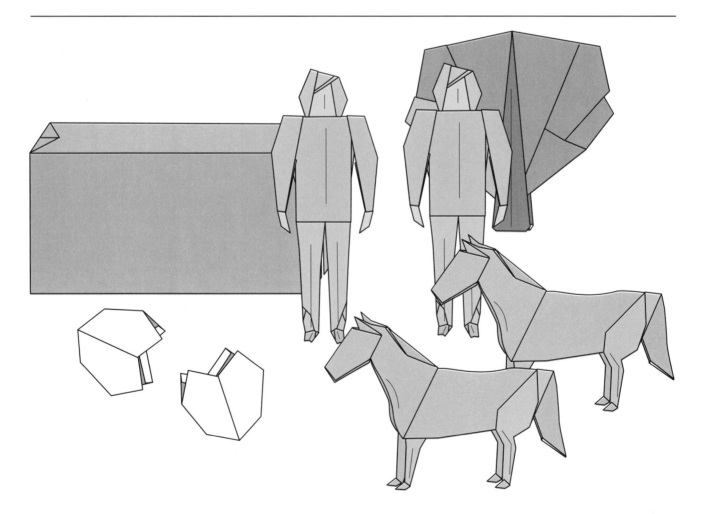

Humpty Dumpty

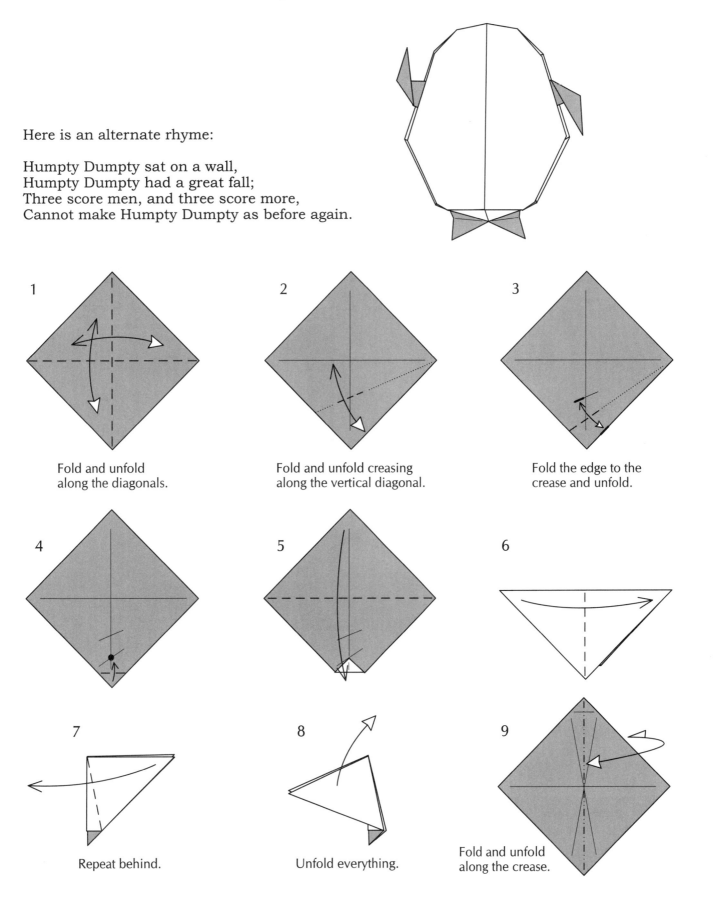

Here is an alternate rhyme:

Humpty Dumpty sat on a wall,
Humpty Dumpty had a great fall;
Three score men, and three score more,
Cannot make Humpty Dumpty as before again.

1

Fold and unfold
along the diagonals.

2

Fold and unfold creasing
along the vertical diagonal.

3

Fold the edge to the
crease and unfold.

4

5

6

7

Repeat behind.

8

Unfold everything.

9

Fold and unfold
along the crease.

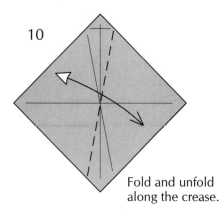

10

Fold and unfold
along the crease.

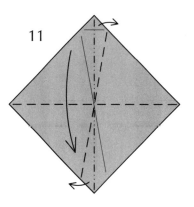

11

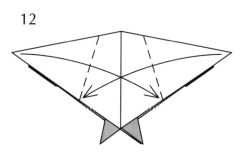

12

Bring the sides, shown with
the bold lines, together.

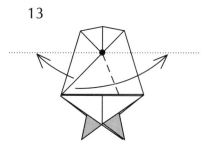

13

Bring the corners up
to form a straight line.

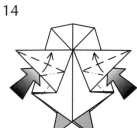

14

Squash folds.

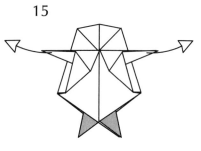

15

Unfold.

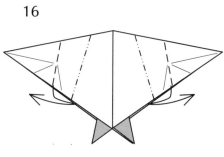

16

Crimp folds.

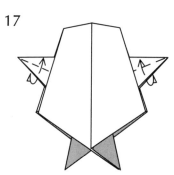

17

Make four squash folds, two
in front and two behind. Fold
along hidden creases.

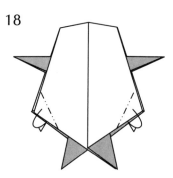

18

Fold inside. Repeat behind.

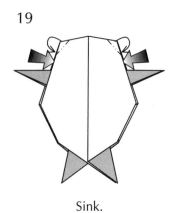

19

Sink.

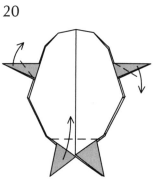

20

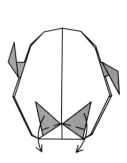

21

Bring the legs in front so
the model can balance.

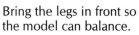

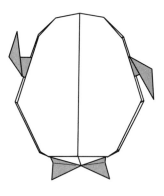

22

Humpty Dumpty

Cracked Egg

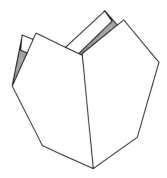

The rhyme *Humpty Dumpty* is a riddle. Can you guess what Humpty Dumpty is? Today we all know it is an egg, of course!

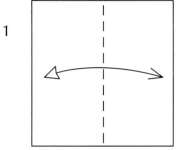

1

Fold and unfold.

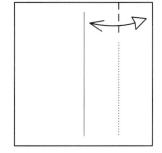

2

Fold and unfold at the top.

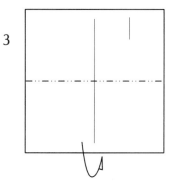

3

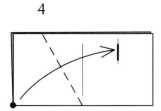

4

Bring the corner to the crease.

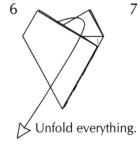

5

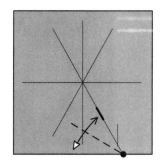

6

Unfold everything.

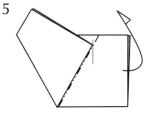

7

Fold and unfold.

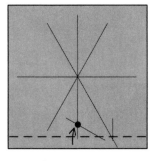

8

Rotate 180°.

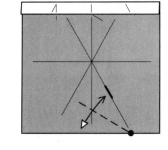

9

Repeat steps 7–8.

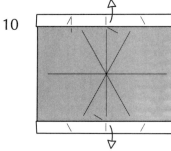

10

Unfold.

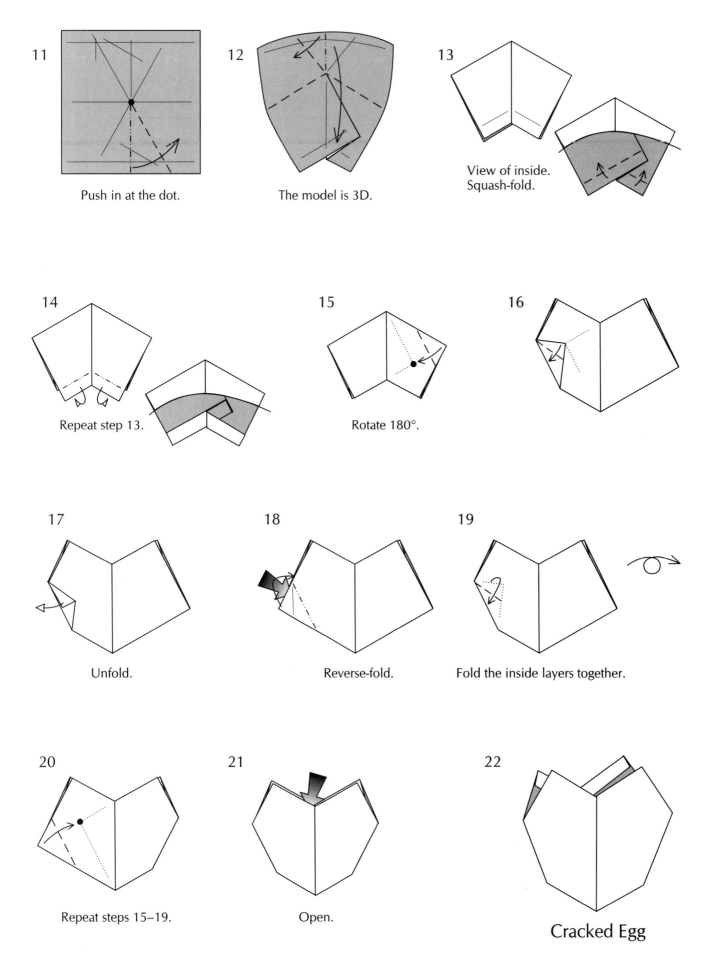

11 Push in at the dot.

12 The model is 3D.

13 View of inside. Squash-fold.

14 Repeat step 13.

15 Rotate 180°.

16

17 Unfold.

18 Reverse-fold.

19 Fold the inside layers together.

20 Repeat steps 15–19.

21 Open.

22 Cracked Egg

Wall

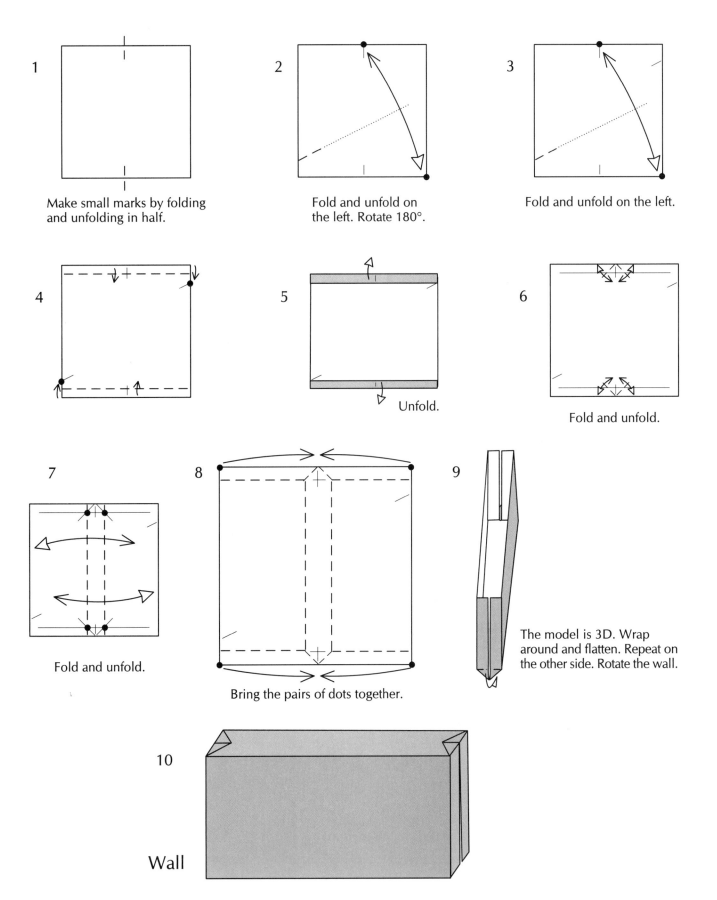

1 Make small marks by folding and unfolding in half.

2 Fold and unfold on the left. Rotate 180°.

3 Fold and unfold on the left.

4

5 Unfold.

6 Fold and unfold.

7 Fold and unfold.

8 Bring the pairs of dots together.

9 The model is 3D. Wrap around and flatten. Repeat on the other side. Rotate the wall.

10 Wall

King's Horse

Here is yet another variation:

Humpty Dumpty sat on a wall,
Humpty Dumpty had a great fall,
Not all the king's horses, nor all the king's men,
Could set Humpty Dumpty up again.

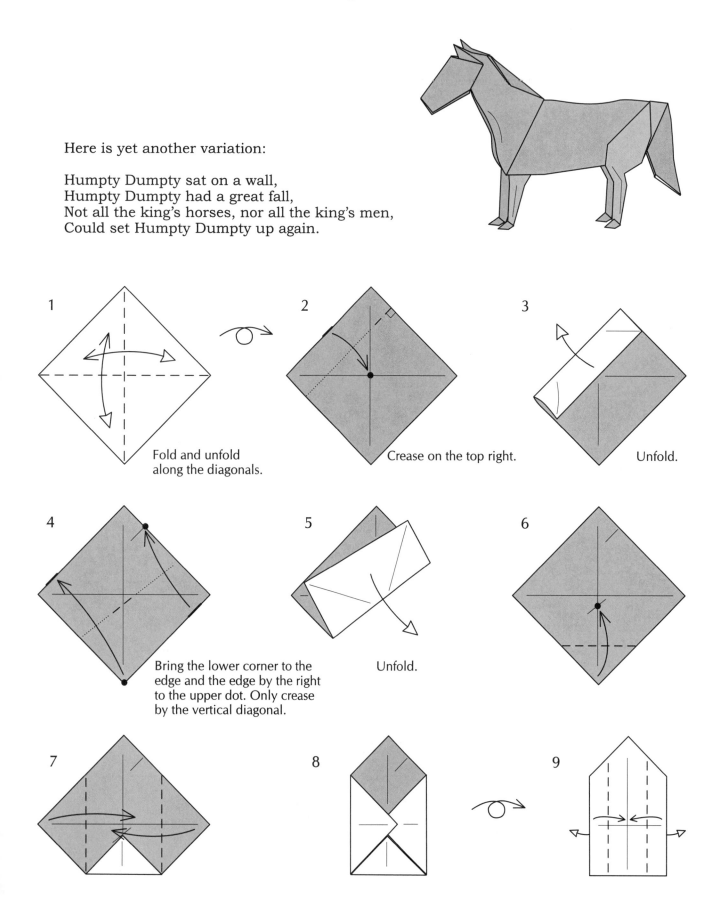

1

Fold and unfold
along the diagonals.

2

Crease on the top right.

3

Unfold.

4

Bring the lower corner to the
edge and the edge by the right
to the upper dot. Only crease
by the vertical diagonal.

5

Unfold.

6

7

8

9

10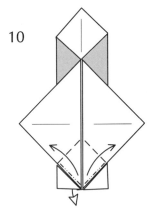

Petal-fold.

11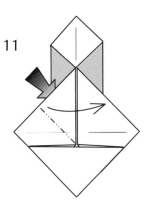

Pull out.

12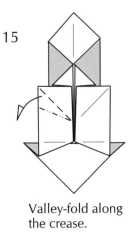

Squash-fold.

13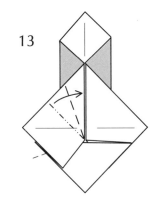

Squash-fold.

14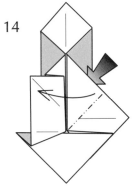

Repeat steps 11–13
on the right.

15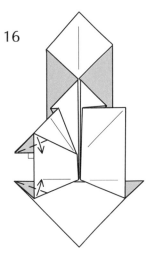

Valley-fold along
the crease.

16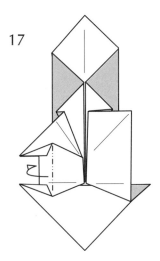

Note the right angle.

17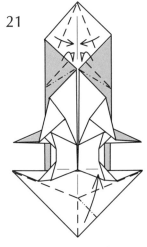

Spread to fold underneath.

18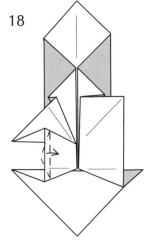

Make a thin petal fold.

19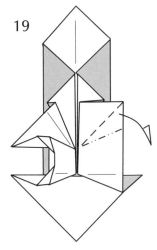

Repeat steps 15–18
on the right.

20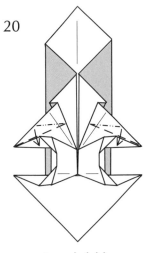

Squash-folds.

21

Rabbit-ear at the bottom.

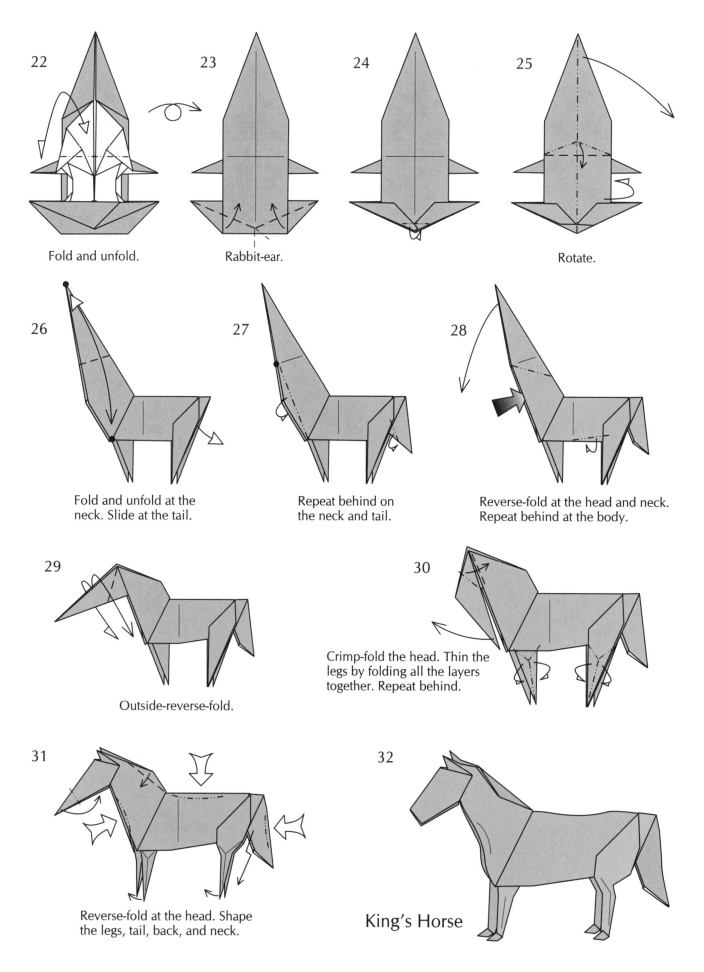

22 Fold and unfold.

23 Rabbit-ear.

24

25 Rotate.

26 Fold and unfold at the neck. Slide at the tail.

27 Repeat behind on the neck and tail.

28 Reverse-fold at the head and neck. Repeat behind at the body.

29 Outside-reverse-fold.

30 Crimp-fold the head. Thin the legs by folding all the layers together. Repeat behind.

31 Reverse-fold at the head. Shape the legs, tail, back, and neck.

32 King's Horse

King's Man

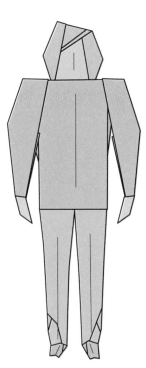

Here is one of several suggested origins to Humpty Dumpty. During the English Civil War (1642-1649) there was a cannon named Humpty Dumpty. It was placed on top of St. Mary's Wall Church in Colchester to protect the city. The enemy hit the tower and Humpty Dumpty fell to the ground. The King's men were not able to mend it.

1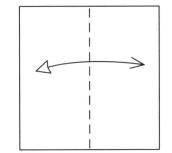

Fold and unfold.

2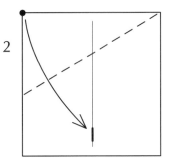

Bring the corner to the line.

3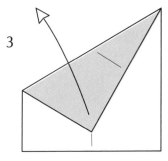

Unfold.

4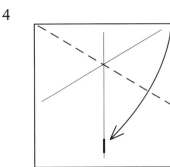

5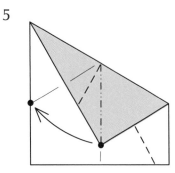

6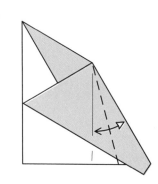

Fold and unfold.

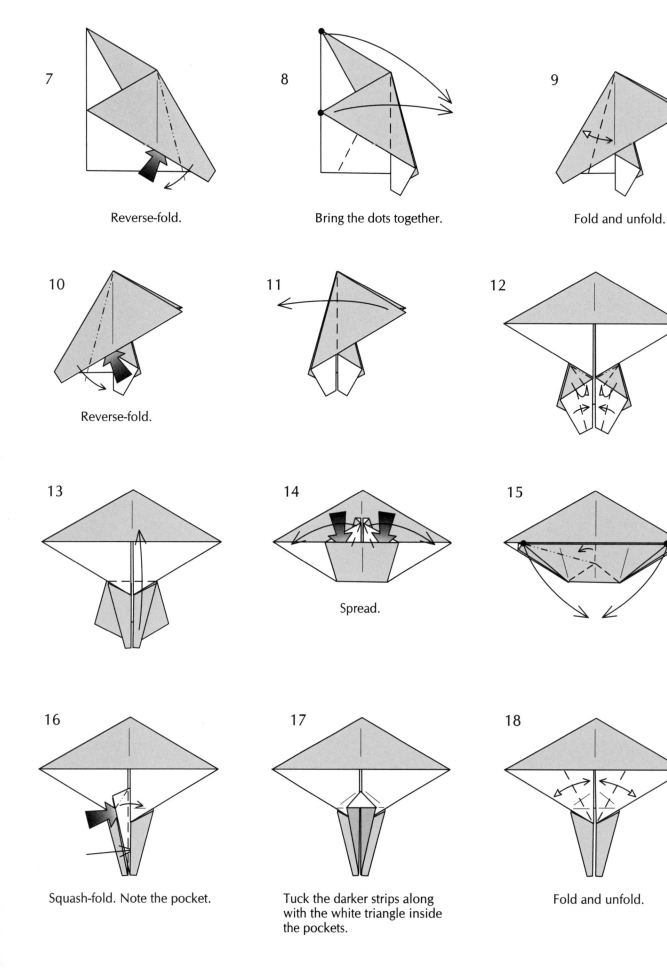

7

Reverse-fold.

8

Bring the dots together.

9

Fold and unfold.

10

Reverse-fold.

11

12

13

14

Spread.

15

16

Squash-fold. Note the pocket.

17

Tuck the darker strips along
with the white triangle inside
the pockets.

18

Fold and unfold.

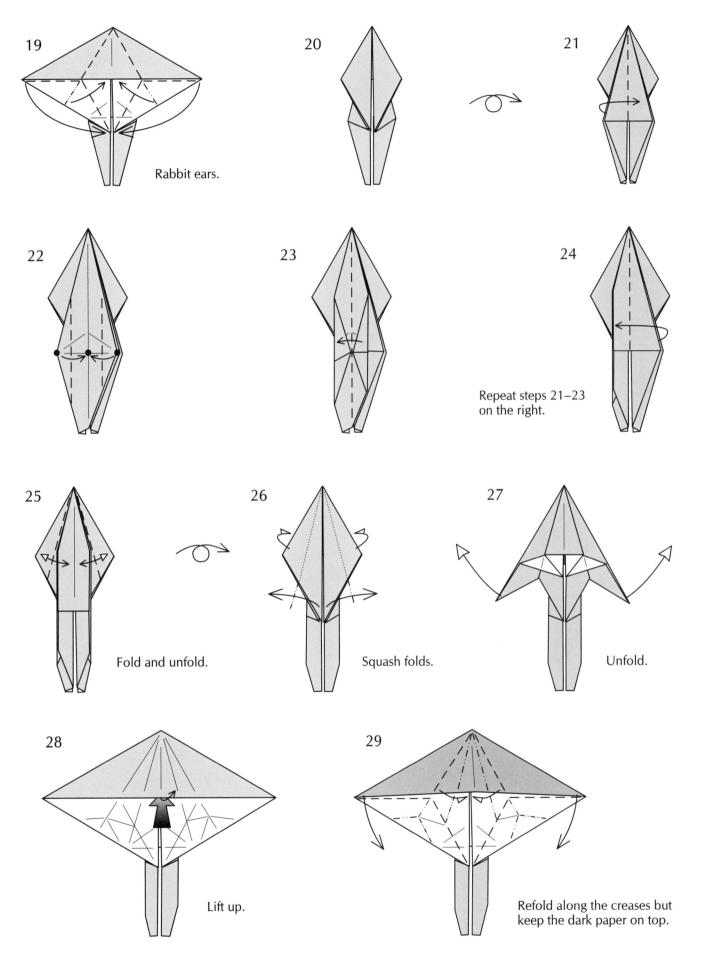

19

Rabbit ears.

20

21

22

23

24

Repeat steps 21–23
on the right.

25

Fold and unfold.

26

Squash folds.

27

Unfold.

28

Lift up.

29

Refold along the creases but
keep the dark paper on top.

30

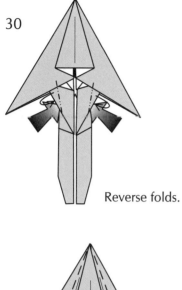

Reverse folds.

31

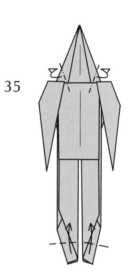

32

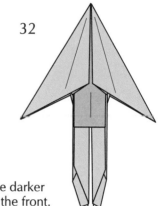

Bring the darker
layer to the front.

33

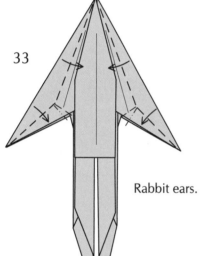

Rabbit ears.

34

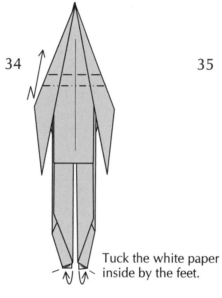

Tuck the white paper
inside by the feet.

35

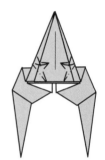

View from behind.

36

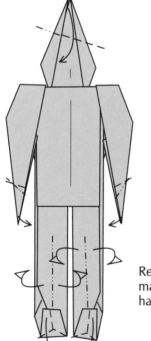

Reverse-fold at the head,
make squash folds for the
hands, and shape the legs.

37

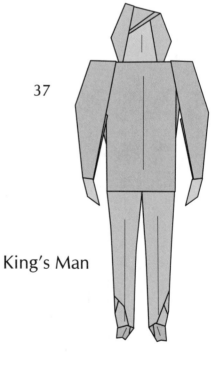

King's Man

Cinderella

Once upon a time in a faraway kingdom, there lived a young woman named Cinderella. Cinderella lived in the cellar of a small house with her stepmother and two stepsisters. The stepmother and stepsisters were very mean, and treated Cinderella very badly. She had to wash and mend their clothes, cook their food and keep their house clean, and instead of having her own room like the others, she had to sleep on a dusty old rug next to the sooty fireplace in the cellar.

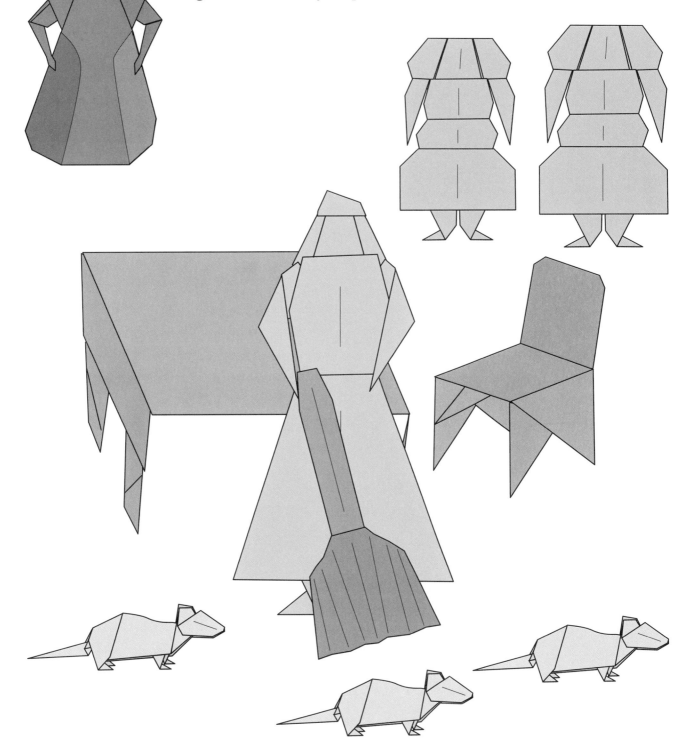

Cinderella

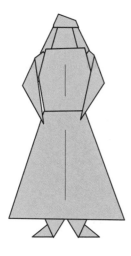

Before

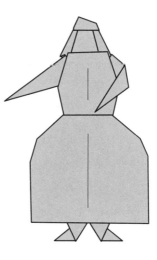

After, with gown.

While Cinderella dreamed of being a princess with beautiful gowns, her stepsisters laughed at her and told her she belonged in the cellar amongst the soot and the mice.

One day, news spread across the kingdom that the king and queen wanted their son, Prince Charming, to get married. To help him find his princess, they were throwing a magnificent ball and would invite all the young women in the kingdom who were not married. The prince would meet them all, and would, they hoped, choose the most beautiful one to be his princess.

1

Fold and unfold.

2

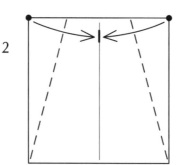

3

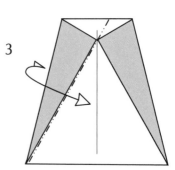

Fold and unfold.

4

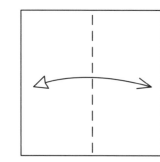

Fold and unfold.

5

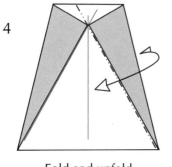

Unfold.

6

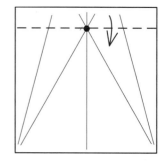

7

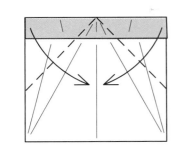

8

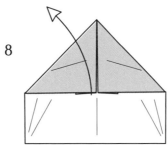

Unfold.

9

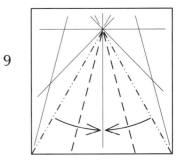

Mountain-fold
along the creases.

10

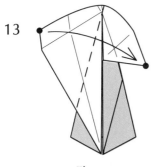

Flatten.

11

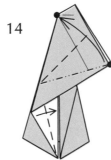

Squash-fold. Valley-fold
along the creases.

12

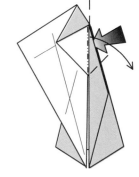

Squash-fold.

13

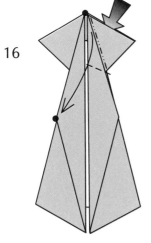

Flatten.

14

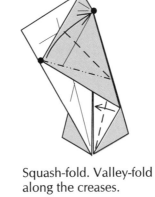

Repeat steps 11–12.

15

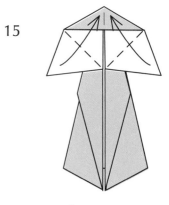

16

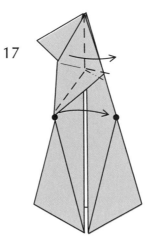

Squash-fold.

17

18

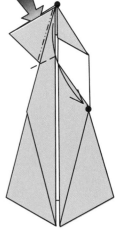

Repeat steps
16–17 on the left.

Cinderella 83

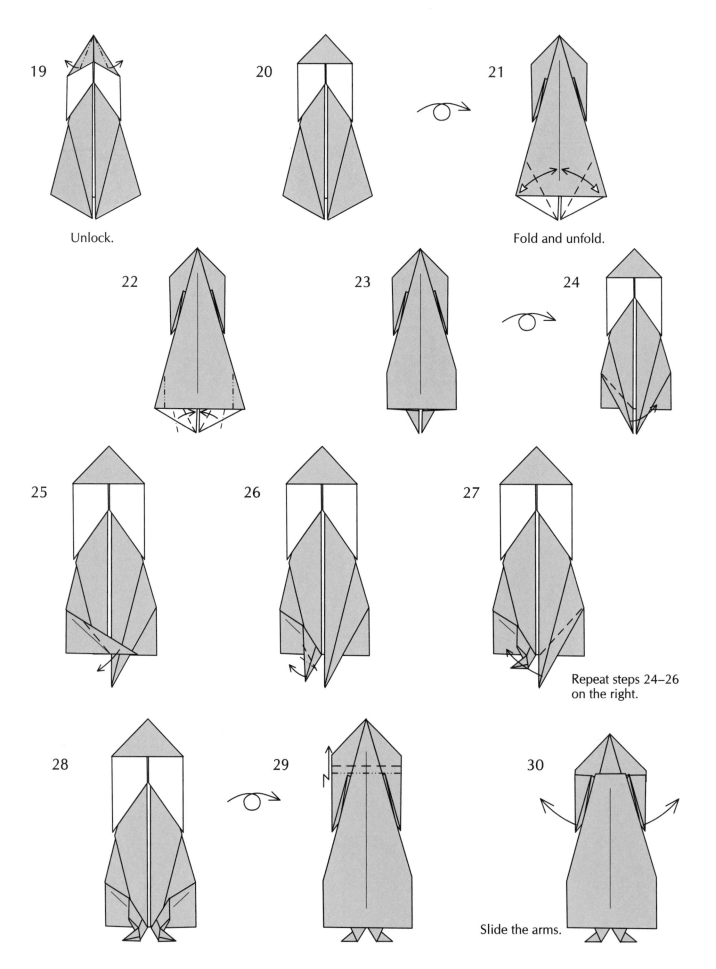

19

Unlock.

20

21

Fold and unfold.

22

23

24

25

26

27

Repeat steps 24–26 on the right.

28

29

30

Slide the arms.

31

32

33

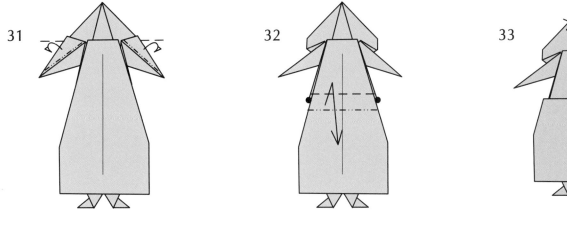

Before

34

35

Before

Cinderella

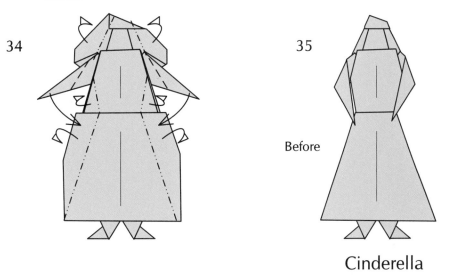

After, with gown.

36

37

After

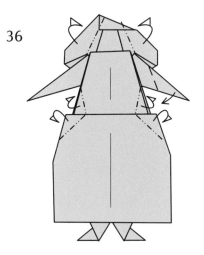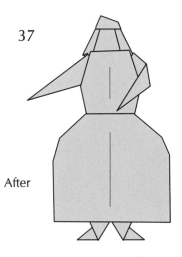

Cinderella

Stepmother

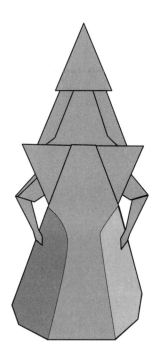

One day, there was a knock on the door of Cinderella's house. She answered the door, and it was the King's messenger carrying an invitation for the two stepsisters.

Cinderella gave her stepmother the invitation, and the stepmother gathered the stepsisters together and showed it to them. They laughed and danced and told Cinderella that she had to sew some new, beautiful gowns for them to wear to the ball. When Cinderella asked if she could go, they all laughed at her and said, "No prince would want a princess who wears torn old dresses and has filthy little mice as her only friends! You are NOT going to the ball!"

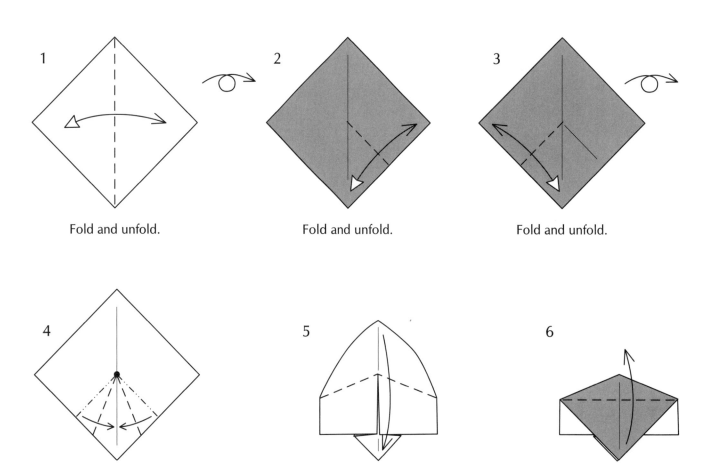

1. Fold and unfold.

2. Fold and unfold.

3. Fold and unfold.

4. Push in at the dot.

5. The model is 3D.

6.

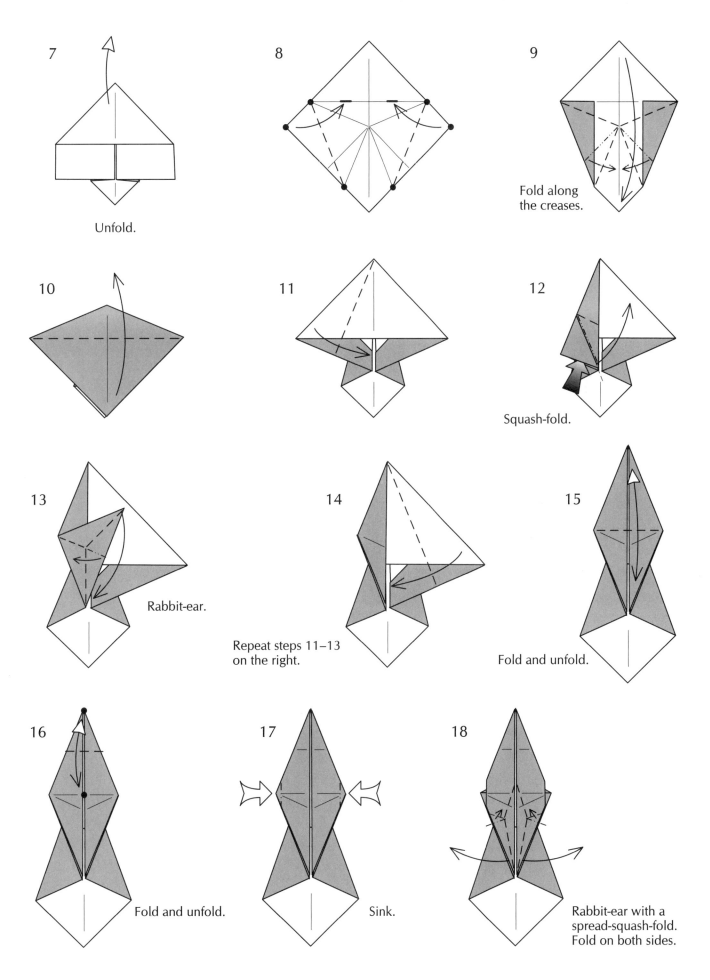

7

Unfold.

8

9

Fold along
the creases.

10

11

12

Squash-fold.

13

Rabbit-ear.

14

Repeat steps 11–13
on the right.

15

Fold and unfold.

16

Fold and unfold.

17

Sink.

18

Rabbit-ear with a
spread-squash-fold.
Fold on both sides.

Stepmother 87

19

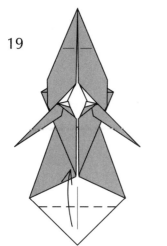

20

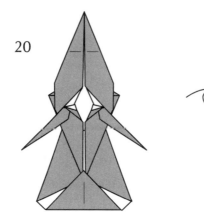

21

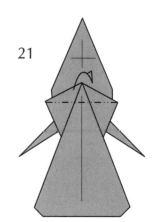

22

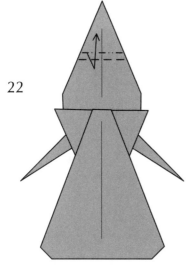

Mountain-fold
along the crease.

23

Crimp-fold the arms.

24

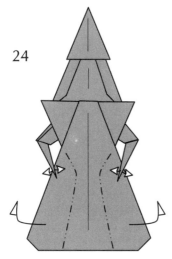

Spread at the hands.
The model can stand.

25

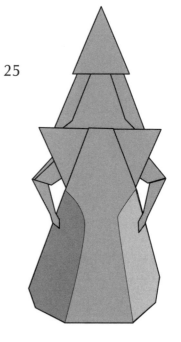

Stepmother

Stepsister

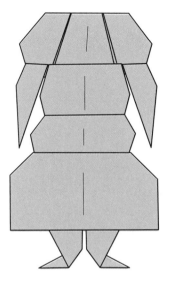

Cinderella was really disappointed, but she set to designing and sewing the gowns for her stepsisters. The gowns were beautiful and the stepsisters were very happy with their new clothes. Still, they teased Cinderella, and reminded her that they were going to the ball and she wasn't.

1

2

Fold and unfold creasing lightly.

3

4

5

6

7

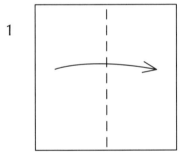

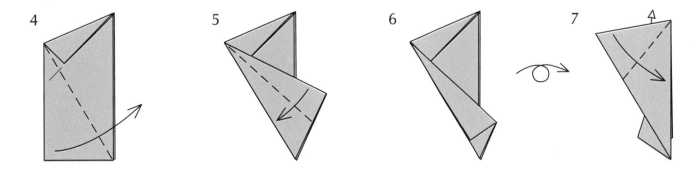

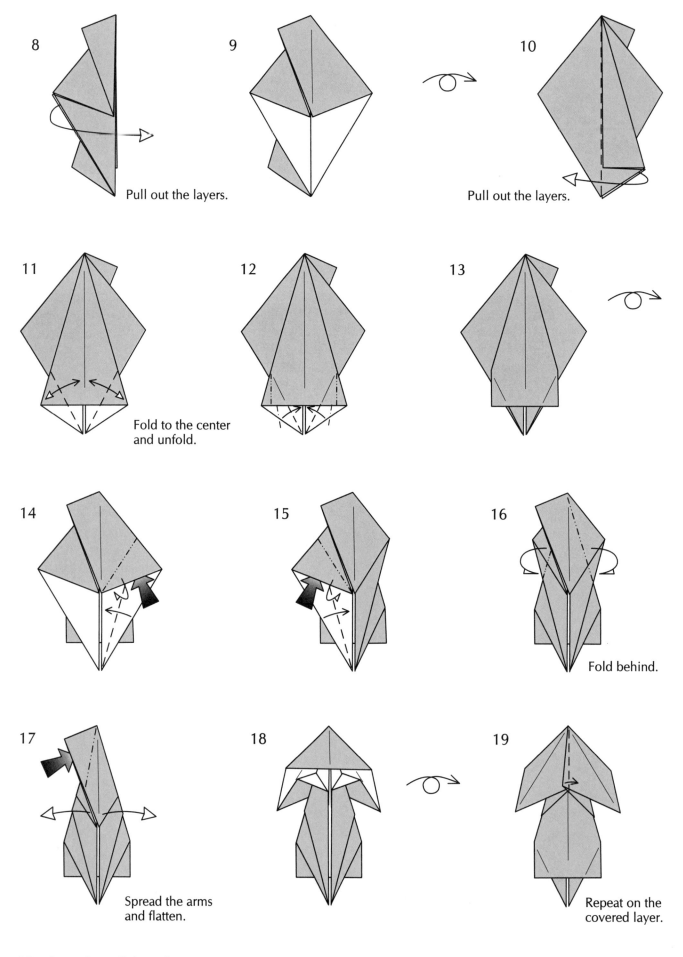

8 Pull out the layers.

9

10 Pull out the layers.

11 Fold to the center and unfold.

12

13

14

15

16 Fold behind.

17 Spread the arms and flatten.

18

19 Repeat on the covered layer.

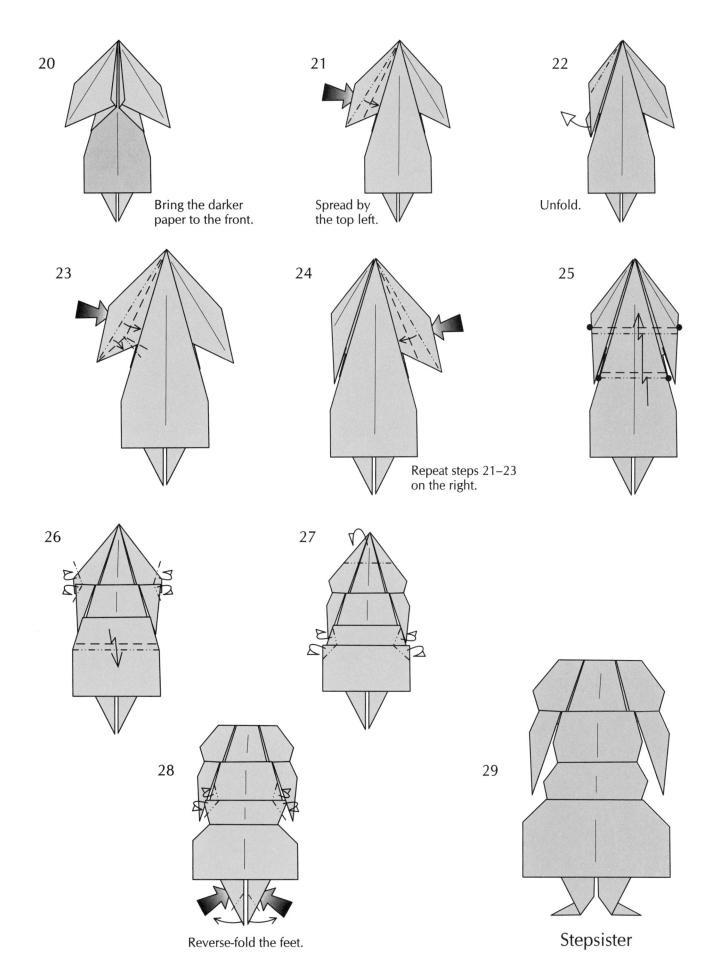

20

Bring the darker
paper to the front.

21

Spread by
the top left.

22

Unfold.

23

24

Repeat steps 21–23
on the right.

25

26

27

28

Reverse-fold the feet.

29

Stepsister

Broom

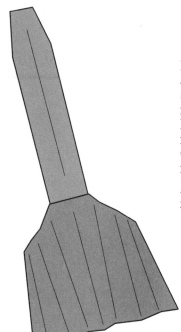

It was the night of the ball, and the whole kingdom was abuzz with excitement. All the mothers accompanied their single daughters to the castle, where they were welcomed into the grand ballroom. A huge, sparkling chandelier hung from the ceiling, and the King's orchestra played the most beautiful music the kingdom had ever heard. Prince Charming began to meet each family and set out to look for his new princess.

Back at the house, Cinderella sobbed as she picked up a broom to sweep the floor.

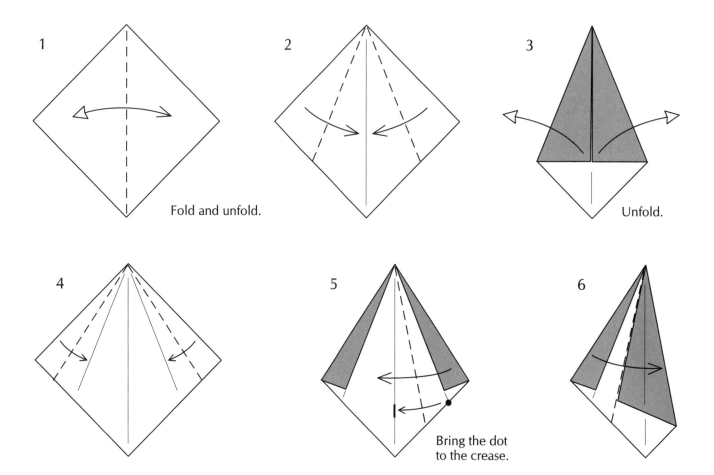

1

Fold and unfold.

2

3

Unfold.

4

5

Bring the dot to the crease.

6

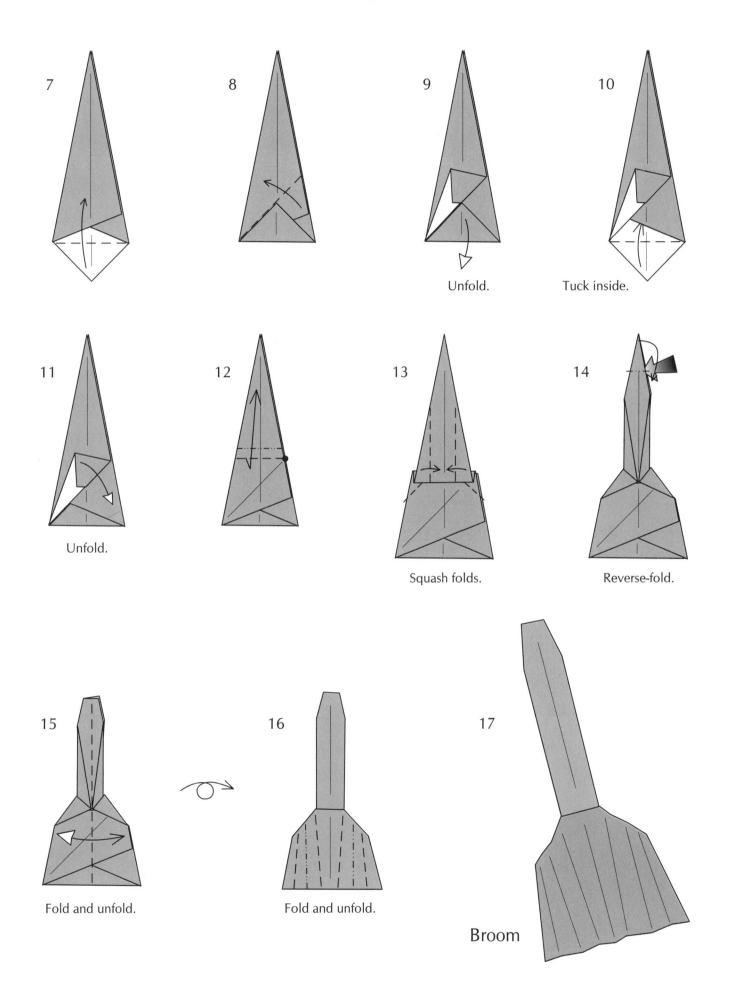

7

8

9

Unfold.

10

Tuck inside.

11

Unfold.

12

13

Squash folds.

14

Reverse-fold.

15

Fold and unfold.

16

Fold and unfold.

17

Broom

Fairy Godmother

Cinderella sat huddled against the fireplace in the cellar, crying and wishing she could go to the ball. She was startled by a noise. It sounded like the beating of wings, and she looked around the room. Above the mantle there appeared what looked like a thousand fireflies, and the shimmering lights became brighter and brighter. There was a big flash of light, and out of the light appeared a kindly old woman. "Who are you?" asked Cinderella. "I am your Fairy Godmother, " said the woman. "I know you wanted to go the ball, but your stepmother and stepsisters wouldn't allow it. I'm here to help make your wish come true!"

Begin with step 19 of Cinderella.

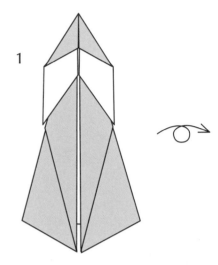

1

2

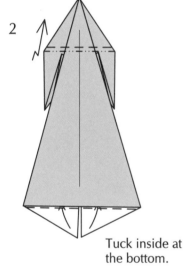

Tuck inside at the bottom.

3

Slide the arms.

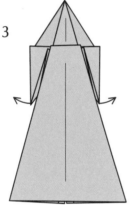

4

5

Make thin reverse folds at the bottom.

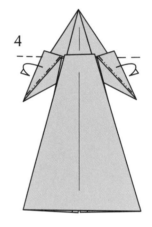

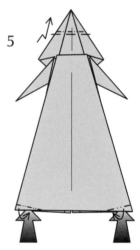

6

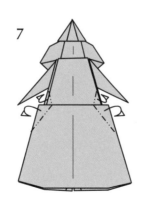

7

8

Fairy Godmother

Mouse

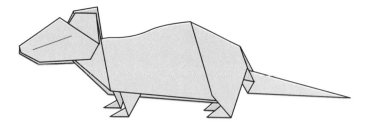

Cinderella stood up, and as she stood next to the fireplace, the Fairy Godmother waved her magic wand. Suddenly a hundred mice came running to Cinderella's feet. The Fairy Godmother whispered to the mice, and they all ran about the house, upstairs and downstairs, and when they came back to the cellar, they were carrying the most beautiful gown Cinderella had ever seen. The girl mice led Cinderella to her bath and cleaned all the soot from her hair and her clothes, and soon she was ready to put on her new gown. As she stood in the gown, she felt wonderful. "Oh," said the Fairy Godmother, "We mustn't forget your shoes!" There appeared on Cinderella's feet a pair of lovely glass slippers.

Begin with step 13 of the Squirrel.

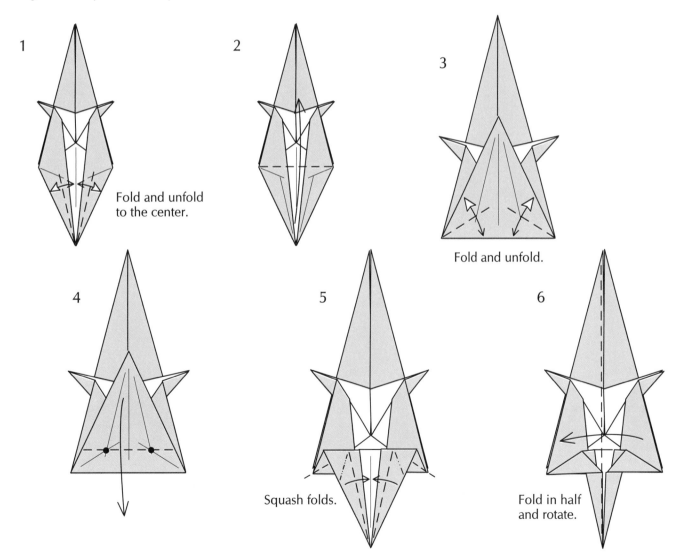

1

2

Fold and unfold
to the center.

3

Fold and unfold.

4

5

Squash folds.

6

Fold in half
and rotate.

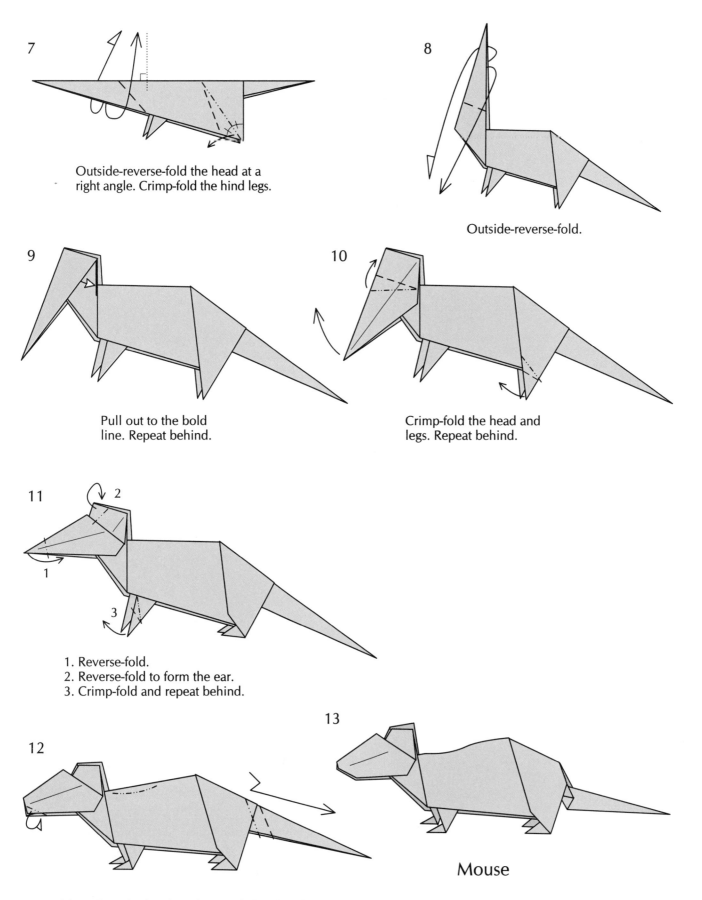

7

Outside-reverse-fold the head at a
right angle. Crimp-fold the hind legs.

8

Outside-reverse-fold.

9

Pull out to the bold
line. Repeat behind.

10

Crimp-fold the head and
legs. Repeat behind.

11

1. Reverse-fold.
2. Reverse-fold to form the ear.
3. Crimp-fold and repeat behind.

12

Fold inside at the head, and repeat behind. Make
reverse folds at the tail, and shape the back.

13

Mouse

Pumpkin

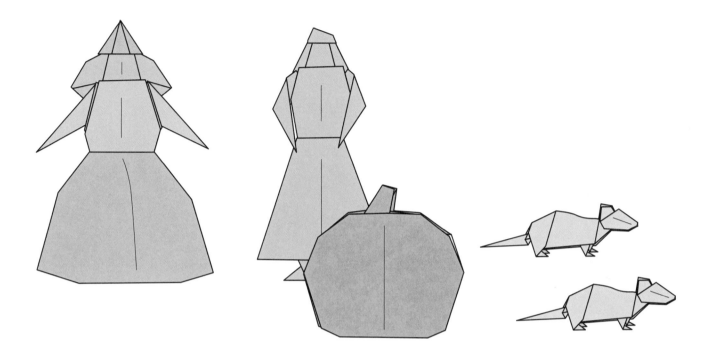

The Fairy Godmother waved her wand and she and Cinderella were suddenly standing outside. Some of the mice came outside and when the wand was waved again, they turned into a team of elegant horses. Another wave of the wand, and a pumpkin that had been growing in the yard turned into a golden coach. A mouse who had been next to the pumpkin became a coachman dressed in the finest livery.

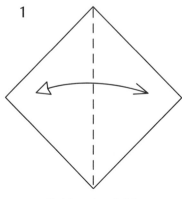

1

Fold and unfold.

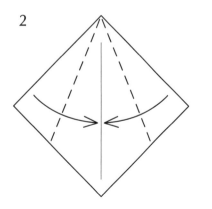

2

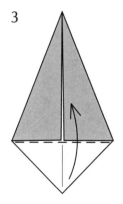

3

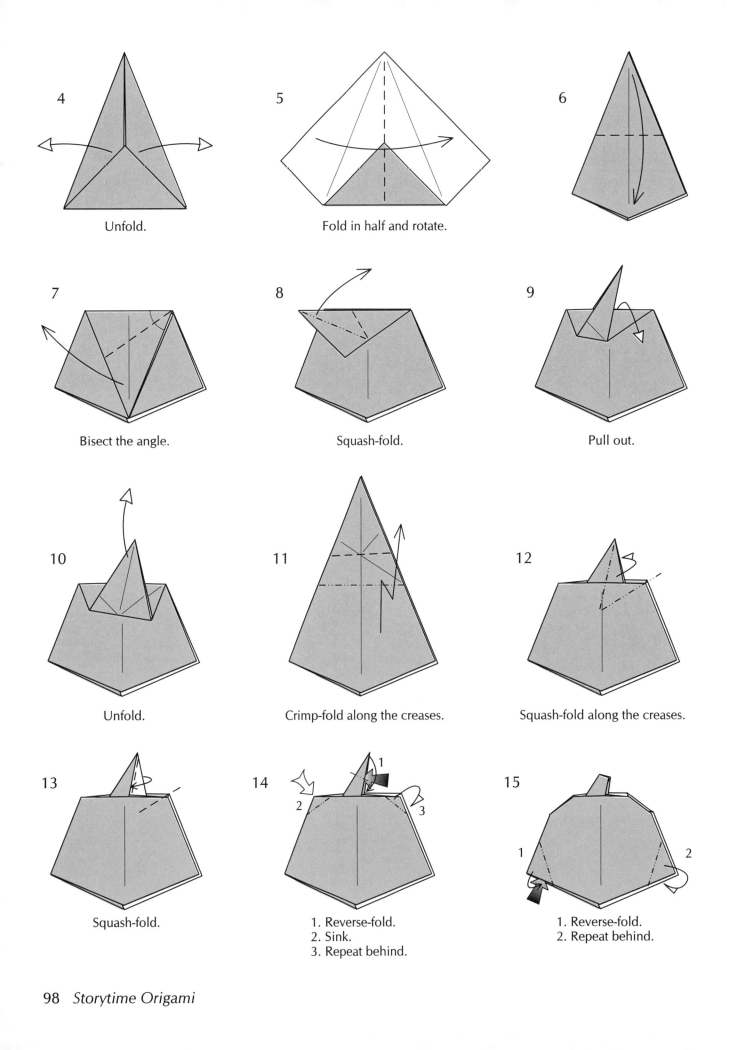

4 Unfold.

5 Fold in half and rotate.

6

7 Bisect the angle.

8 Squash-fold.

9 Pull out.

10 Unfold.

11 Crimp-fold along the creases.

12 Squash-fold along the creases.

13 Squash-fold.

14
1. Reverse-fold.
2. Sink.
3. Repeat behind.

15
1. Reverse-fold.
2. Repeat behind.

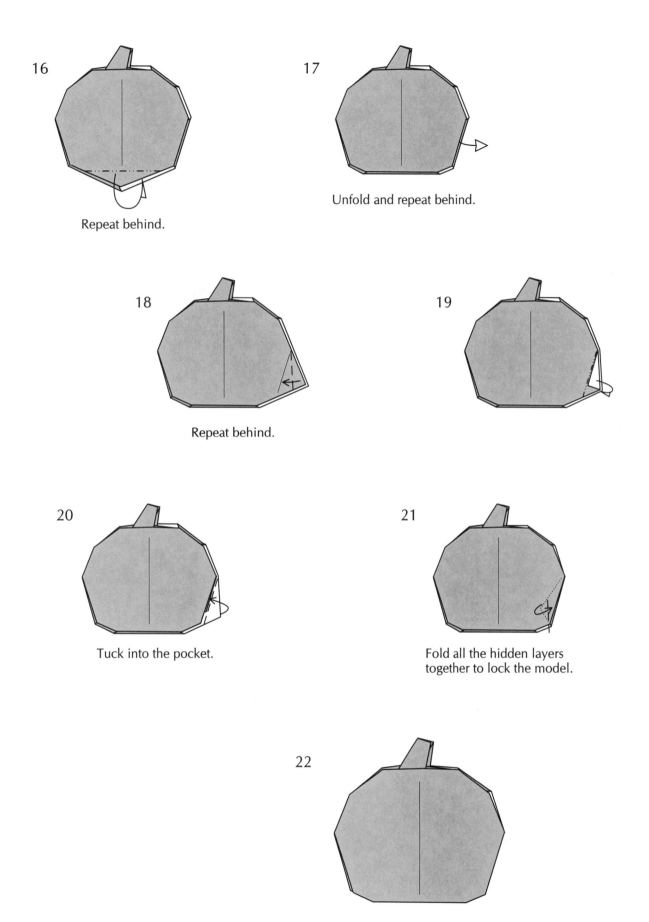

16

Repeat behind.

17

Unfold and repeat behind.

18

Repeat behind.

19

20

Tuck into the pocket.

21

Fold all the hidden layers together to lock the model.

22

Pumpkin

Carriage

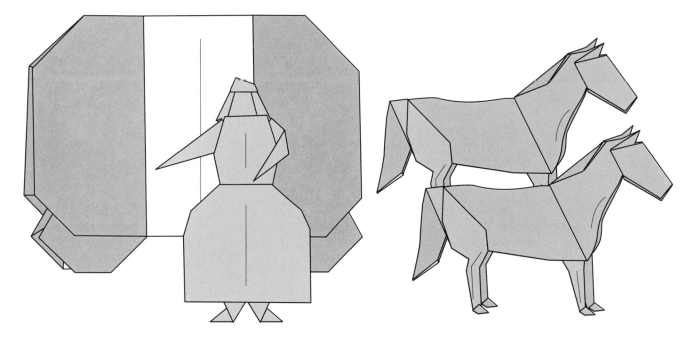

The Fairy Godmother said, "You are ready to go to the ball. But you know, all this is magic, and will not last forever. You may go to the ball and have a wonderful evening, but you must be back home by the stroke of midnight. At midnight, your coach will turn back into a pumpkin, the horses and driver will turn back into mice, and your gown will turn back into your old clothes." "I promise I'll be back by midnight," said Cinderella, and off she went to the ball.

1
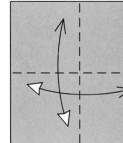

Fold and unfold.

2

Fold and unfold.

3

Bring the dot to the crease.
Only crease at the top.

4
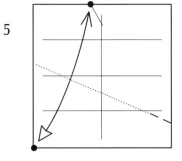

Unfold.

5
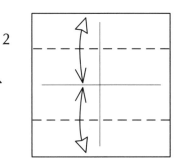

Fold and unfold
creasing on the right.

6
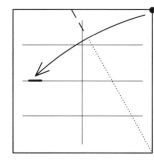

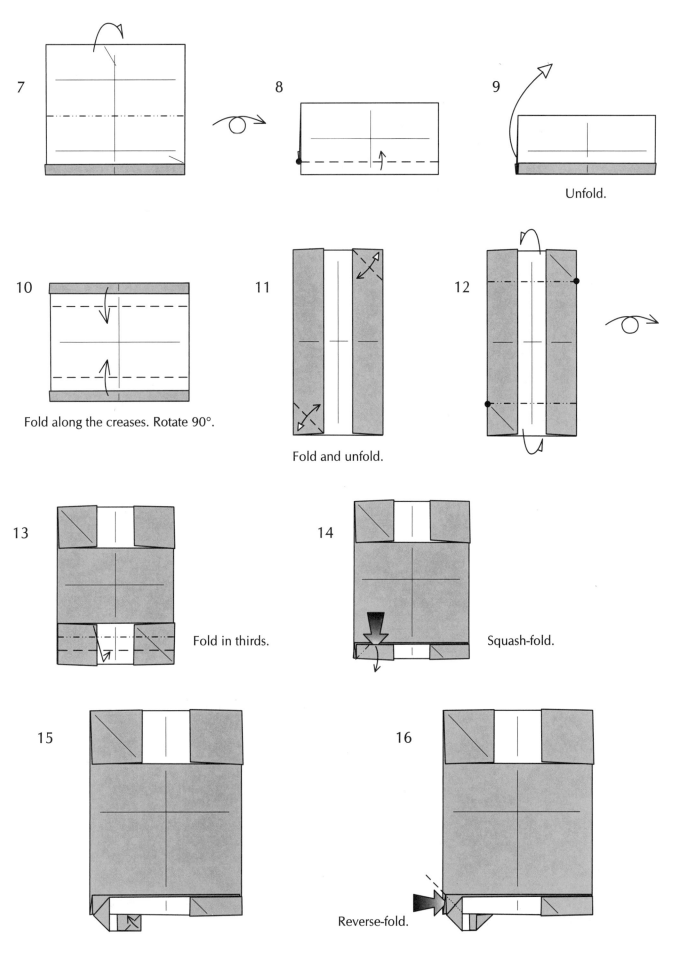

7

8

9

Unfold.

10

Fold along the creases. Rotate 90°.

11

Fold and unfold.

12

13

Fold in thirds.

14

Squash-fold.

15

16

Reverse-fold.

17

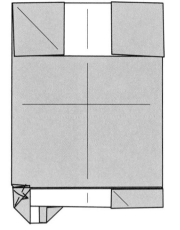

18

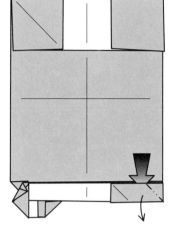

Repeat steps 14–17
on the right.

19

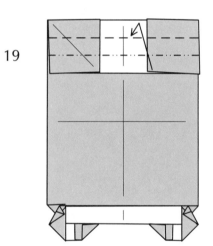

Repeat steps 14–18 at the top.

20

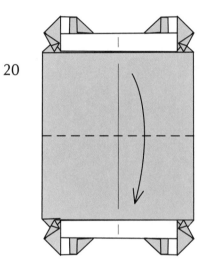

21

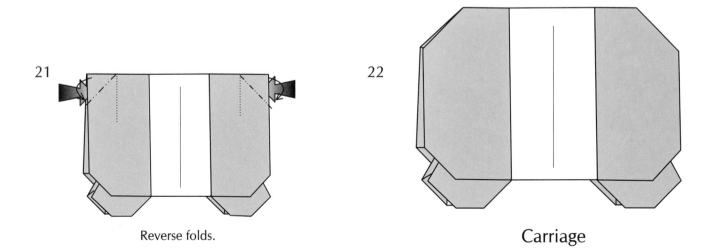

Reverse folds.

22

Carriage

Throne

Prince Charming was dancing with yet another young woman from the kingdom when he heard the doors of the ballroom open. There, standing at the top of the grand staircase in a glowing white gown, was Cinderella. The music stopped and everyone in the ballroom turned to look. Mesmerized, the Prince left the woman with whom he had been dancing, and walked towards Cinderella. Cinderella started down the stairs, and the two met in the middle. The music began and Cinderella and Prince Charming walked together, hand in hand, to the center of the ballroom. They danced the most elegant waltz, and all the others whispered to each other. "Who is she?" "Where did she come from?" "Now he won't look at any of us!" Indeed, Prince Charming was no longer interested in anyone else in the room but Cinderella. They danced again and again throughout the evening, and in her joy, Cinderella forgot something the Fairy Godmother had said.

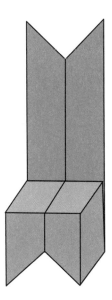

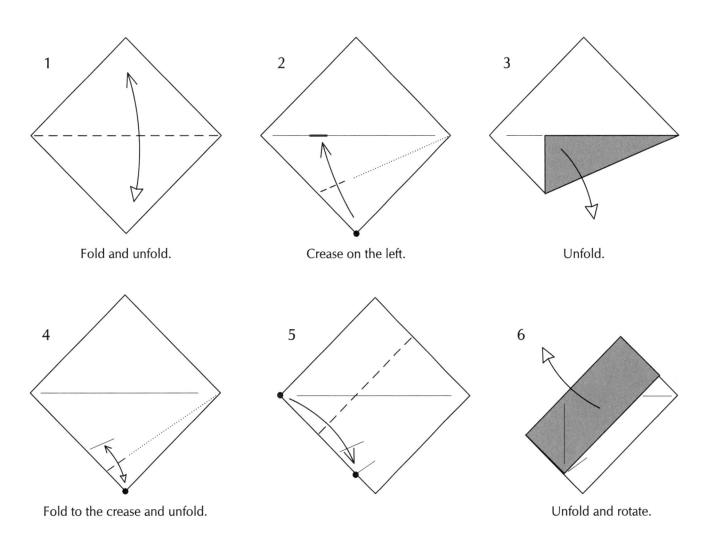

1. Fold and unfold.

2. Crease on the left.

3. Unfold.

4. Fold to the crease and unfold.

5.

6. Unfold and rotate.

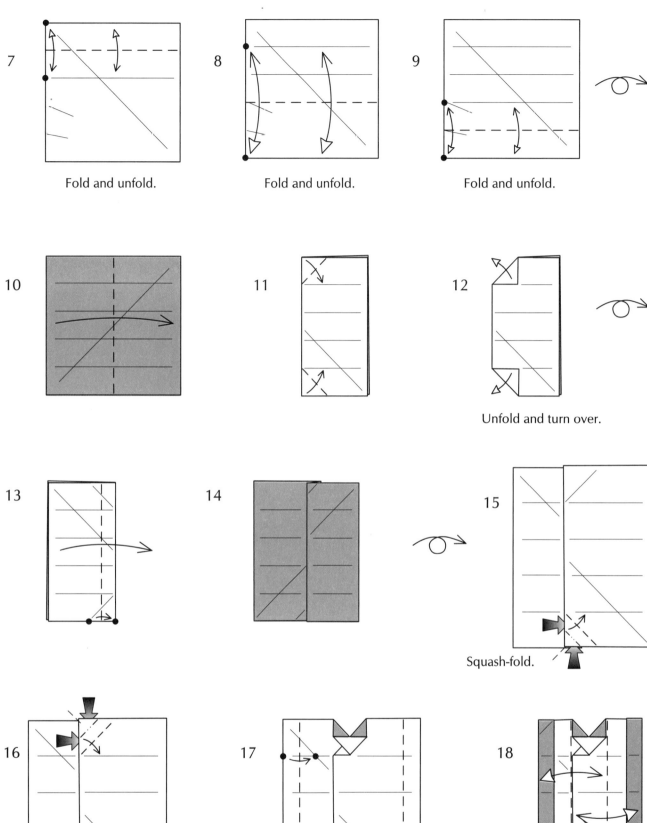

7 Fold and unfold.

8 Fold and unfold.

9 Fold and unfold.

10

11

12 Unfold and turn over.

13

14

15 Squash-fold.

16 Squash-fold.

17 Note the pocket at the bottom.

18 Fold and unfold.

19

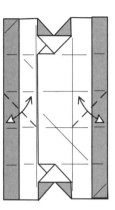

Fold and unfold.

20

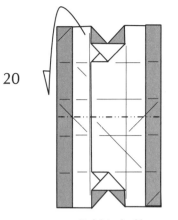

Fold in half.

21

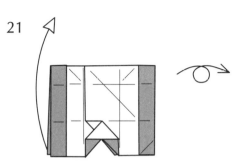

Unfold and turn over.

22

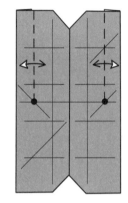

Fold and unfold.

23

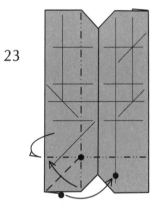

Puff out at the upper dot. Bring the lower dot to the front.

24

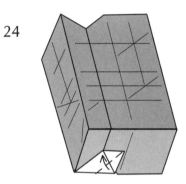

25

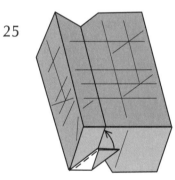

26

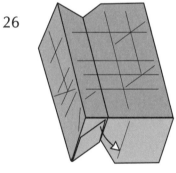

Unfold.

27

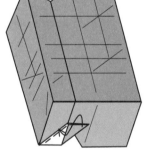

Tuck inside the pocket. (See step 17.)

28

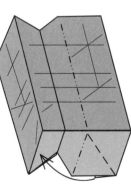

Repeat steps 23–27 on the right.

29

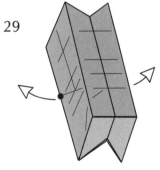

Spread and flatten on both sides.

30

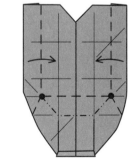

Push in at the dots.

31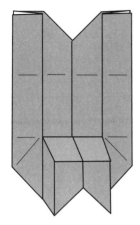

32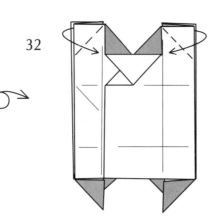

33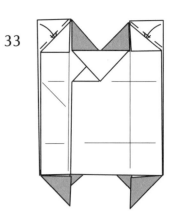

Tuck inside.

34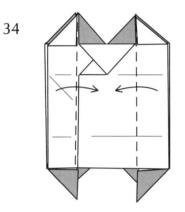

35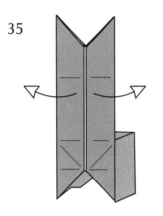

Unfold.

36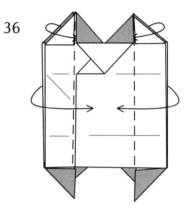

Tuck the upper layer inside.

37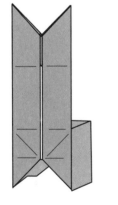

38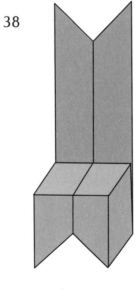

Throne

Clock

As the clock began to strike Twelve, Cinderella suddenly remembered the Fairy Godmother's words. She tore herself away from the Prince and ran toward the stairs. "Where are you going?" pleaded the Prince. "What is your name? Will I ever see you again?" But Cinderella was already out of the castle, running toward her coach. Just as she got to the coach, the final chime of the clock rang midnight, and the coach turned back into a pumpkin, and the coachman and horses turned back into mice. Cinderella's gown was once again a tattered, dusty dress. But something was missing! In her haste, Cinderella had left one of her glass slippers on the stairs in the ballroom.

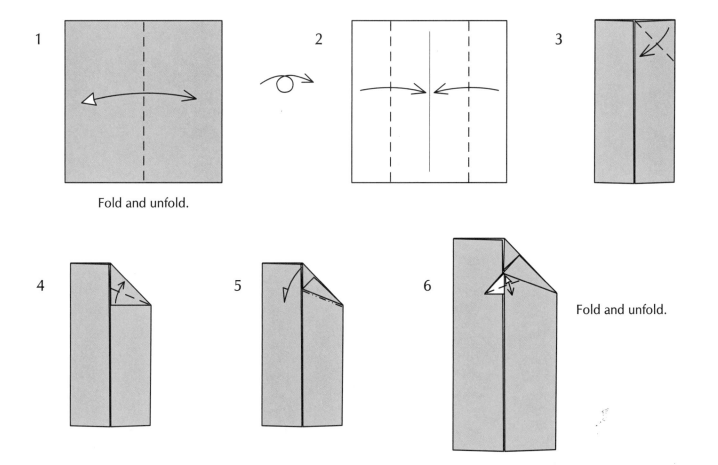

1

Fold and unfold.

2

3

4

5

6

Fold and unfold.

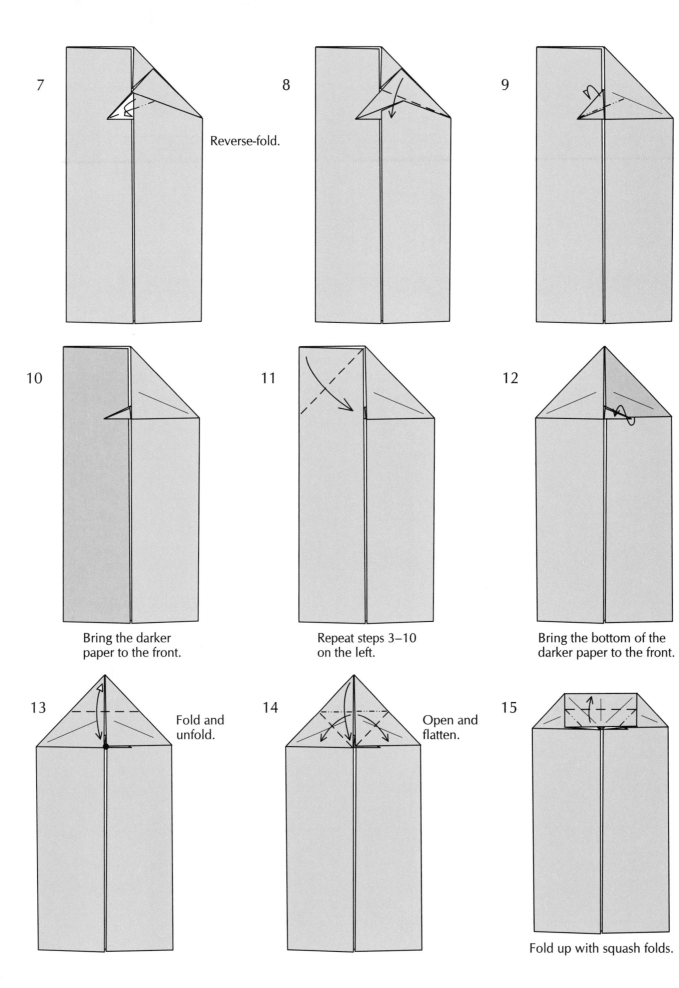

7

Reverse-fold.

8

9

10

Bring the darker
paper to the front.

11

Repeat steps 3–10
on the left.

12

Bring the bottom of the
darker paper to the front.

13

Fold and
unfold.

14

Open and
flatten.

15

Fold up with squash folds.

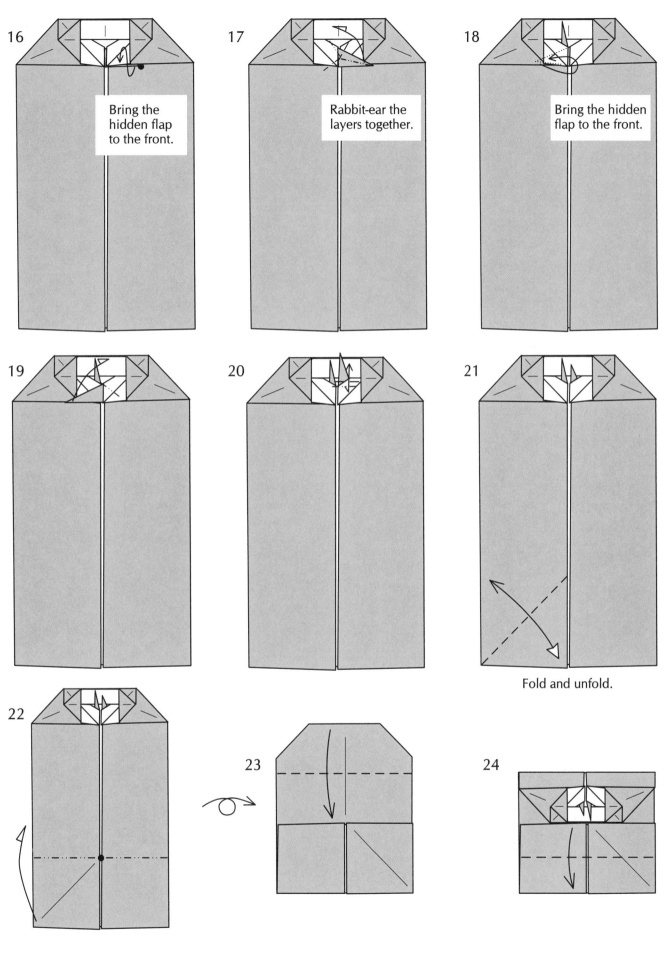

16 Bring the hidden flap to the front.

17 Rabbit-ear the layers together.

18 Bring the hidden flap to the front.

19

20

21 Fold and unfold.

22

23

24

25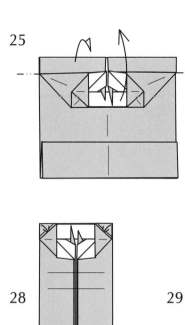

26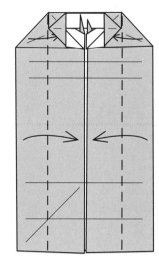

Unfold.

27 Tuck inside at the top.

28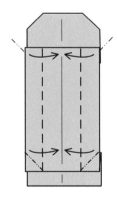

Tuck inside at the top.

29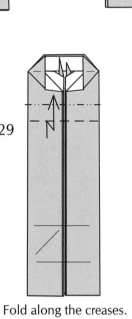

Fold along the creases.

30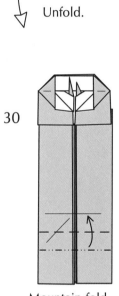

Mountain-fold along the crease.

31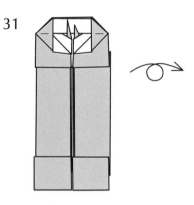

32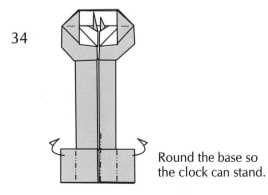

Squash folds.

33

34

Round the base so the clock can stand.

35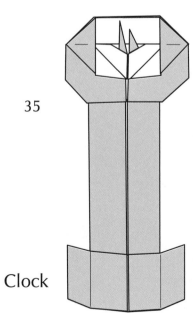

Clock

King

The next day, news went around the kingdom that Prince Charming had met his princess at the ball, but she had left before he could find out her name. The Prince was going to search throughout the kingdom for his princess and the way he would find her was by having each woman who was at the ball try on the glass slipper that was left on the stairs. If it fit someone, he would know he had found his princess.

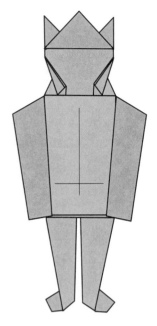

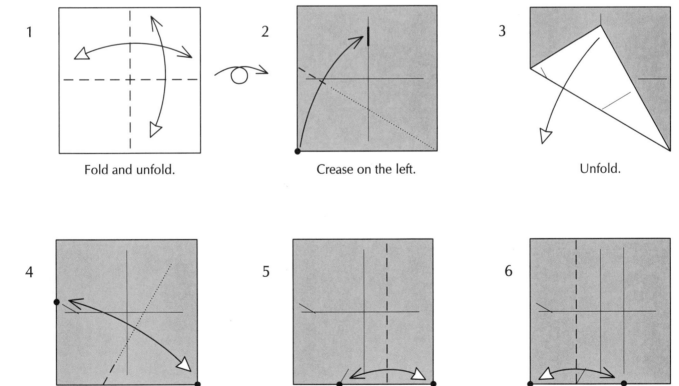

1 Fold and unfold.

2 Crease on the left.

3 Unfold.

4 Fold and unfold at the bottom.

5 Fold and unfold.

6 Fold and unfold.

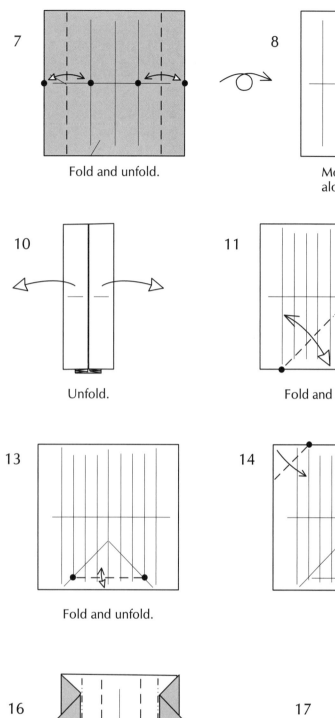

7 Fold and unfold.

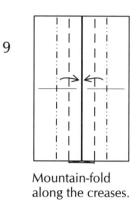

8 Mountain-fold along the creases.

9 Mountain-fold along the creases.

10 Unfold.

11 Fold and unfold.

12 Fold and unfold.

13 Fold and unfold.

14

15

16

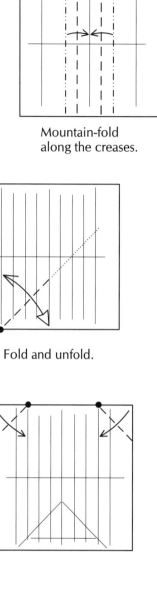

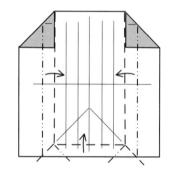

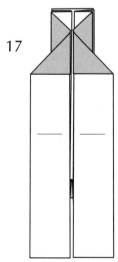

17

18 Reverse folds.

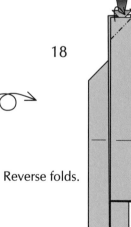

19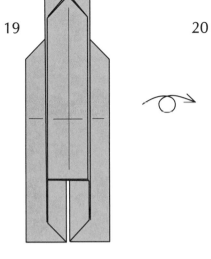

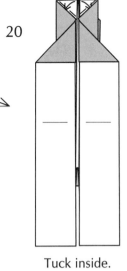 20

Tuck inside.

21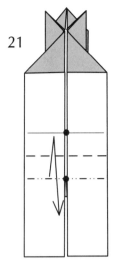

The dots will meet.

22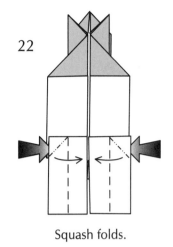

Squash folds.

23

24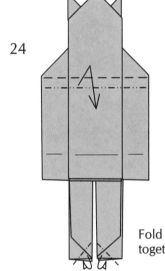

Fold all the layers
together at the feet.

25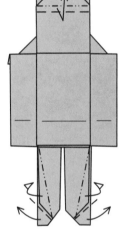

26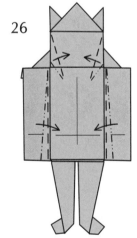

27

28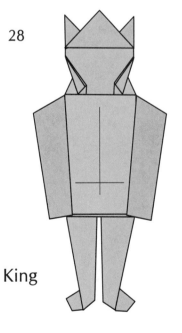

King

Queen

The Prince and his valet visited house after house, and nobody seemed to fit the glass slipper. Many young women tried to stuff their feet into it, or put something into it so their foot wouldn't slip out, but it simply wouldn't fit anyone. Finally, after a week of searching, there was one more house to visit.

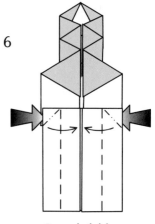

Begin with step 11 of the King.

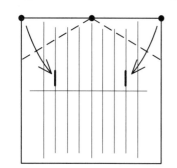

1

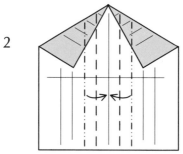

2

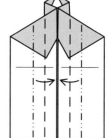

3

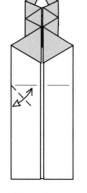

4

Fold and unfold.

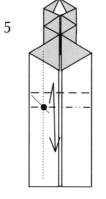

5

6

Squash folds.

7

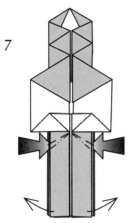

Place your finger into the lower layer. Spread the layers together.

8

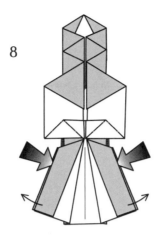

Spread the top layers.

9

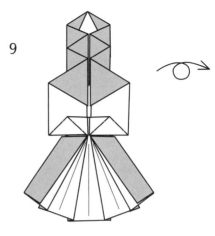

10

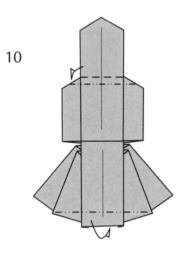

11

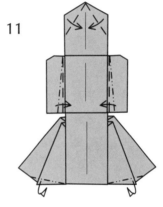

12

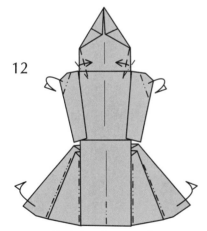

Curl the dress so the Queen can balance.

13

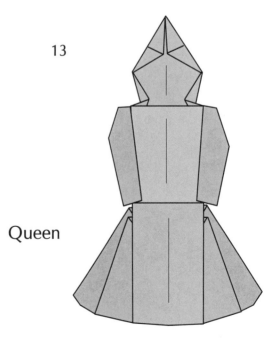

Queen

Prince

There was a knock at the door of Cinderella's house. She answered the door and let the Prince in, but since she was all dusty, he didn't recognize her. The stepmother immediately sent her down to the cellar, and called the two stepsisters to meet the Prince. They giggled and tried to impress him, but he had a strong feeling none of these would be the woman he'd met at the ball. After he tried to fit the glass slipper on their feet, he knew he had failed to find his princess. He was about to leave the house when a mouse scurried onto his foot. He tried to kick it away, but the mouse held on, and looked up at him. "I think it's trying to tell me something," he said. The stepmother kicked the mouse away and said, "Oh, that's just a mouse from the cellar. Don't pay any attention to that." "The cellar..." said the Prince. "Didn't you send someone down to the cellar when I came in?" "Oh, that's just Cinderella. Don't bother with her. She's just our housemaid." But the Prince knew this was his last chance, the last woman left in the kingdom for him to meet. So against the protests of the stepmother and the stepsisters, he went downstairs to the cellar.

Begin with step 17 of the King.

1

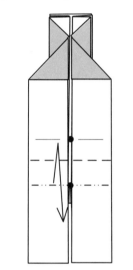

Continue with steps 21 to the end of the King but omit the folds for the head in step 25.

2

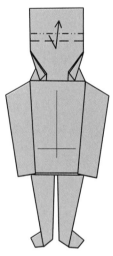

3

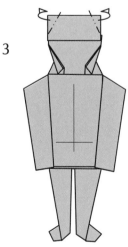

4

Prince

Glass Slipper

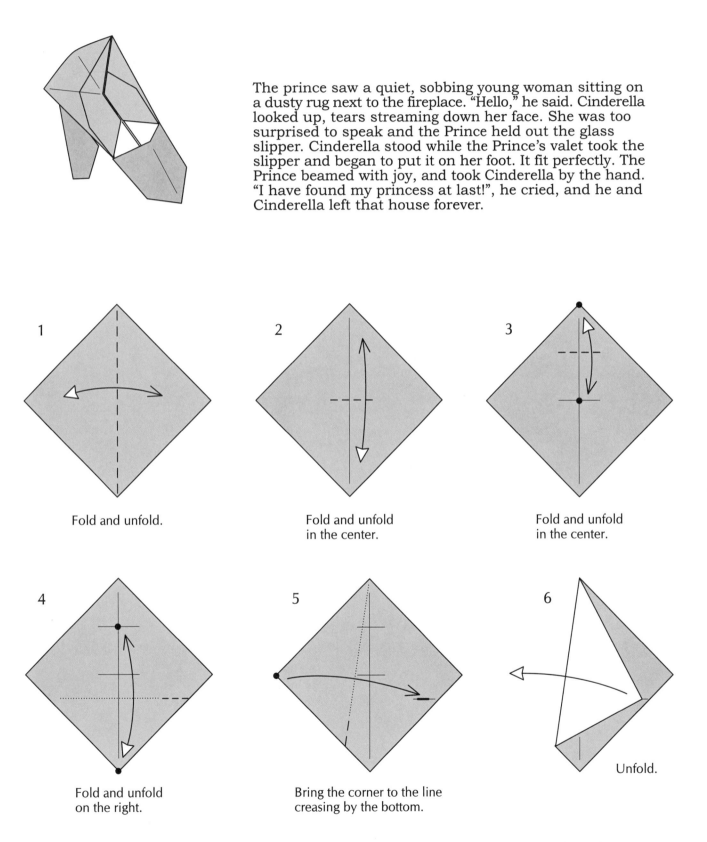

The prince saw a quiet, sobbing young woman sitting on a dusty rug next to the fireplace. "Hello," he said. Cinderella looked up, tears streaming down her face. She was too surprised to speak and the Prince held out the glass slipper. Cinderella stood while the Prince's valet took the slipper and began to put it on her foot. It fit perfectly. The Prince beamed with joy, and took Cinderella by the hand. "I have found my princess at last!", he cried, and he and Cinderella left that house forever.

1

Fold and unfold.

2

Fold and unfold
in the center.

3

Fold and unfold
in the center.

4

Fold and unfold
on the right.

5

Bring the corner to the line
creasing by the bottom.

6

Unfold.

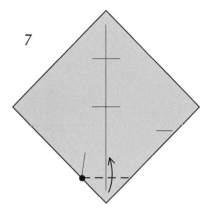

7

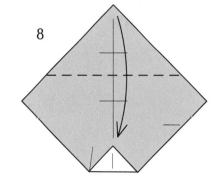

8

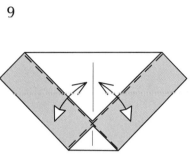

9

Fold and unfold.

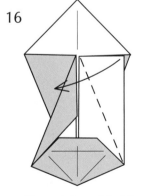

10

Unfold.

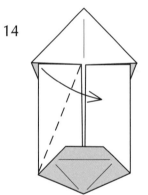

11

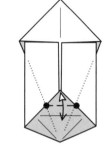

12

Fold and unfold.

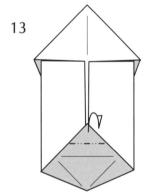

13

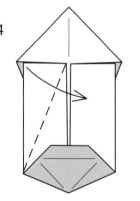

14

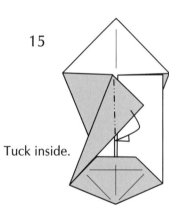

15

Tuck inside.

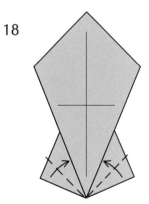

16

Repeat steps 14–15
on the right.

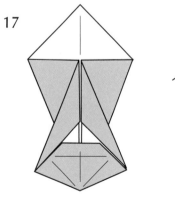

17

18

19

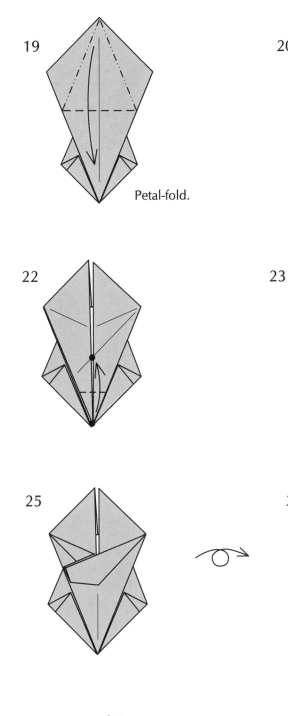

Petal-fold.

20

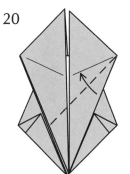

21

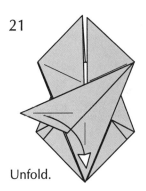

Unfold.

22

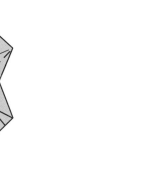

23

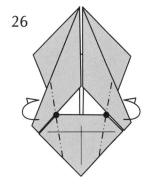

Rabbit-ear.

24

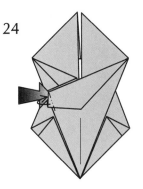

Reverse-fold.

25

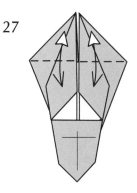

26

27

Fold and unfold.

28

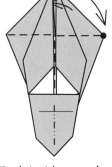

Tuck inside to make
the slipper 3D.

29

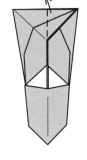

Curve the back.

30

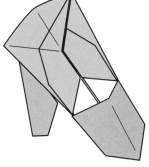

Glass Slipper

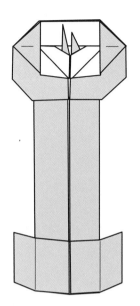

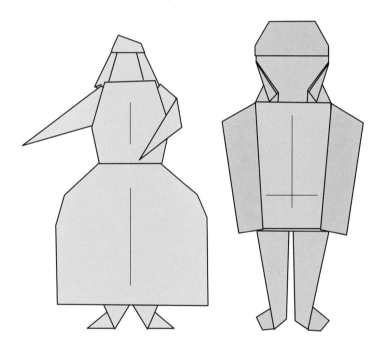

The wedding of Prince Charming and Cinderella was the most beautiful the kingdom had ever seen, and everyone was invited. Everyone, that is, except for Cinderella's stepmother and stepsisters. They were sent away from the kingdom, never to return again. As for Prince Charming and Cinderella? They lived happily ever after.